Small Space Style

weldon**owen**

Small Space Style

BECAUSE YOU DON'T NEED TO LIVE LARGE TO LIVE BEAUTIFULLY

WHITNEY LEIGH MORRIS
of The Tiny Canal Cottage

weldon**owen**

CONTENTS

EATING

SLEEPING

BATHING

To my mom, dad, and sister, who taught me that it's the people and the experiences, not the stuff. To Lindsay, Nell, and Emily for proving my family's lesson true. And to Adam, West, StanLee, and Sophee for living the lesson with me, every day.

The outside may be tiny, but the inside is infinite.

Thank you.

A NOTE FROM WHITNEY

I live in a tiny home. I moved here many years ago, not because I was on a minimizing mission or because it was the "on-trend" thing to do. I don't even consider myself a minimalist per se. I simply fell in love with the space. I had no idea that it would ultimately reroute my professional career, and I certainly didn't expect for it to change my entire outlook on life, which it has.

The Tiny Canal Cottage—as I refer to it—is located along the ocean-fed waterways of Venice Beach, California. It functions as my office and studio, but most importantly, it's a year-round home. My husband, our son, our two rescue beagles, and I all share the space with a genuine joy that somehow continues to grow and evolve.

As a result of social media, generous editorial coverage, and a wide range of brand collaborations over the years, our compact cottage is now known around the world. I often feel as though we've ushered millions of people through our French doors and hosted them in less than 400 square feet (37 sq m). Because, in a way, thanks to the internet and print, we have.

Adam and I got married on the front stoop of our Cottage, and we welcomed our son into this little world shortly thereafter. We've shared these (and many more) extraordinarily personal experiences publicly because, in a time when populations are increasing and profound damage to the planet is evident, we want to show people firsthand that living with less for the long term as a growing family and business in a scaled-down space is not only doable but also delightful.

While I am madly in love with my home, I don't think that this particular space is what has captured everyone's attention. Instead, I believe it's the message that resonates with folks: We don't have to live large to live beautifully.

Living with less is not only a way to save money and reduce our environmental footprint. It can also inspire us to function more efficiently, think more creatively, and be more involved in our communities.

For me, the key to living in a small home or apartment is not figuring out how to Tetris a life's worth of stuff into limited square footage. It's about understanding what you truly need—and don't need—in order to live comfortably and contentedly, day by day. My intention is for this book to help you as you embark upon your own journey into the world of small-space living. I hope that these pages provide you with ideas for crafting a tiny space that feels infinitely beautiful, inspiring, and welcoming for you and your loved ones.

Whitney

LIVING

Living spaces are like our own personal museums, with all our memories on display. Set up this multipurpose room so it functions as well as delights.

001 Create a Warm Welcome

Living in a small space often requires retraining your eye to look at your home's everyday features in new ways. To start, try tackling your entryway—or lack thereof. The design world makes a big to-do about entryways and how they set the tone for the entire residence. Retailers even dedicate entire catalog sections to the items "needed" to pull off a chic and practical landing point for your family and guests. But what can you do if you only have a stoop or a hallway—or absolutely no dedicated area whatsoever? At the Cottage, we've struck upon a streamlined solution that helps us feel organized on our way out and welcomed on our way in—even though we're just working with a modest front step.

RACK UP REMINDERS To one side of our front door, there's a vertical metal rack where I store our collection of woven market totes. (In one of the baskets I keep a 6-foot/1.8-m tarp rolled up that I can throw over the rack when it rains.) A few other items hang here as well, such as a miniature broom and a thermos carrier. When I see the thermos carrier, I remember to grab my beverage so I won't need to buy one when I'm out. And as I pass the baskets, I'm reminded to bring along a container for anything I need to pick up, which encourages me to limit my shopping to only what that container can hold (and thereby control the size and number of items I bring into my home). And of course, it means I can skip a plastic or paper bag if I do make a purchase. The little broom helps us quickly sweep down the stoop. (Since we like to leave the door open for our dogs, StanLee and Sophee, to come and go as they please during the day, it's especially important to keep our front stoop clean.)

MAKE A SHOE-CHANGE STATION On the opposite side of the stoop, there's a small chair where we sit to put on or take off our footwear, and we use it as a spot to momentarily place any items we're carrying as we find our keys.

SET UP A SIMPLE LANDING STRIP Just inside the door is the solution to our remaining entryway needs. On the door itself, two simple wooden thumbtacks hold our keys and a clip with outbound mail. A low jute stool sits against the windows without obstructing them, and this is where I drop my bag when I come home.

MIND THE DETAILS To beautify the stoop, I added a lantern that I light most evenings, plus a small hanging plant. I set up an earthenware water bowl for the pups to visit when they're in the yard, leaving enough space for us to navigate through the doorway. A modern indoor-outdoor rug sits on the top step in lieu of a doormat.

002 Find a Place to Hang Your Hat

No coat closet? You can easily improvise a landing strip for outerwear and accessories with a stylish wall rack mounted near your front door. (It helps to add a small hanging mirror to one of the hooks—it'll provide the opportunity for a glance at your reflection before you head out the door—as well as a narrow ledge for your wallet or a small stack of mail.) Keep in mind that tight quarters can feel even tighter when overcrowded with too many objects, patterns, and styles, so curate your items judiciously. If you're hanging something on the wall, it should feel like art! For instance, perhaps you should display your beautiful lightweight gray wool coat by the door, where you'll see it daily, but your bright orange snow jacket should likely wait for winter inside your closet.

003 Decorate Your Door with Essentials

As always, when square footage is at a premium, go vertical. Consider the items that you can suspend (rather than rest on a surface), and outfit your entryway accordingly. You don't need a ring dish for keys—just hang them on a hook or other hardware near (or on) your door. You can also tie string between two hooks, nails, or tacks, and voilà—you've created a place for your sunglasses, too.

When decorating your walls with keys, glasses, or headphones, it's important to inspect them so you maintain a polished look. Is your key ring crowded with old keys and plastic store membership cards? Try relocating the cards to your wallet (or the recycling bin), as well as getting rid of old keys and storing those you rarely use. In a small space where your everyday items are in plain sight, the most minute details make a big difference in your home's overall look.

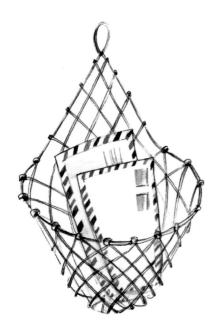

004 Manage Your Mail

So much of keeping a small space uncluttered is to limit what makes it through the front door in the first place—and mail is a huge offender. Start by canceling catalogs (you can subscribe instead to digital newsletters) and removing your name from the credit card list, cutting down on the offers you receive. Second, decline paper correspondence from all banks, credit cards, investments, and healthcare providers, opting instead to receive statements and invoices via email. Then keep your mail from piling up by dedicating a helpful but limited amount of space for your post. Whether you suspend a small basket by the front door, mount a narrow shelf on your wall, or use a clip to hold your envelopes, give yourself the excuse to handle your mail daily rather than letting it pile up. Take a mere three minutes when you get home to scan, recycle, and shred anything you don't need to physically keep, and you'll find that a tiny perch is more than enough for your snail mail.

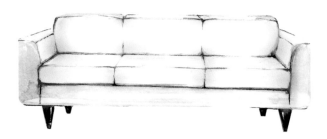

005 Make an Enticing Main Living Space

The living room is a main focal point—if not *the* focal point—of any home. But for tiny apartments and houses, it's frequently one of only two or three rooms, so it has to perform multiple functions within modest square footage. The chameleonlike nature of the small-space living room is one of my favorite parts of living with less. It's incredible what we can all do in limited space when we realize that we don't need more stuff or more room. We just need a touch of creativity.

I refer to the main living space in the Cottage as "the little room that could." It functions as a family room, a dining room, an office, a child's playroom, a guest bedroom, and an extra workspace. The majority of the time, it's set up as the living room, yet even when serving its primary function, it's multitasking just below the surface.

MAKE LARGE FURNITURE DO MORE
One of the best features of the Cottage is its built-in couch. The clever custom design maximizes every inch, providing seating for five, sleeping surfaces for two, and ample storage beneath and on either side of the cushions. With no overstuffed cushions or billowing covers, the sofa takes up no extra visual space.

REACH DEEP FOR STORAGE The removable wooden doors beneath the benches hide a storage area that spans the entirety of the couch. By upcycling wine crates and sliding them like drawers into these spacious cubbies, we created easily accessible shoe storage. Since the compartments are as long as the built-in itself, we are also able to stash longer items such as a spare rug and kraft paper rolls beneath the couch.

KEEP CLOSE BUT CONCEAL Bordering both sides of the couch are built-in shelves that serve as end tables. To one side, open shelving holds wicker baskets for miscellaneous items, such as pet accessories, office supplies, and spare candles. On the opposite side, a cabinet door hides three deep built-in shelves with access to electrical outlets. These shelves hold a full-size cordless vacuum, a wireless printer/scanner, and a large bin containing handbags and backpacks.

See? The little room that could! And all in under 120 square feet (11 sq m).

A deliberate selection of furniture and accessories is key to making a small-scale home livable. In the Cottage, there's simply no room for any piece that has only one purpose! Try these double-duty furnishings and concealed storage ideas, and you'll maximize floor space and eliminate clutter.

006 Conceal in the Coffee Table

Retailers have caught on to the tiny-living craze and now offer several handsome coffee table models that have built-in storage—whether it's a shelf below the tabletop, a surface that folds out to reveal a drawer underneath, or both.

007 Use a Trunk as a Surface

I chose a wicker trunk as our coffee table in the Cottage; it holds our guest bedding, but you could store sports equipment or travel gear inside. I love the natural texture it adds to our space—it shows that storage can be curated to suit your style.

008 Stash Media in a Bench

There's no need to choose between extra seating for guests and storage for your records (or books or catchall baskets). Find a unit that does both. Make sure it's sturdy enough to support the weight of a few friends, and top it off with a cozy cushion.

009 Make Your Couch Do Double Duty

Large furniture pieces are under particular pressure to make the most of their space on the floor plan. Couches with a hidden compartment beneath the seat really earn their keep—just lift up a subtle handle to access additional throw pillows, blankets, or whatever needs hiding.

010 Seek Out a Mirror–Coat Rack Combo

How did it take us so long to discover this efficient and elegant design idea? A simple mirror with hooks and rungs along the side can catch coats, handbags, hats, scarves, and other accessories on your way in the door, as well as let you glimpse your reflection and apply any finishing touches on your way out. It's perfect for displaying your finer apparel items, too.

011 Brighten Up a Table with a Built-In Lamp

Smart lighting is crucial in any home, tiny or not! But why give limited floor or tabletop real estate to a lamp, especially when you may find yourself knocking it over. Instead, try a small side table that's been specially designed to include a baseless light source. This clever idea reduces the lamp's footprint while still providing task lighting for reading or working.

012 Fold Out a Slim Console

I'm a big fan of the slim console table. Stationed in the entryway, living room, or bedroom, these low-profile pieces provide just enough surface for an impromptu desk or a tray for keys, wallets, and sunglasses. Even better are versions that fold out to reveal storage and a bigger surface when you need it for, say, dressing a buffet table or working on a craft project.

013 Bounce Light to Enlarge a Room

Let science help you out: The more you're able to reflect light around a room, the brighter—and therefore larger—that room will appear to be. Here are some tips for boosting illumination.

CHOOSE PALE HUES When you're selecting paint, furniture, or textiles, keep in mind that clean, light colors—such as crisp whites and creamy off-whites— help visually enlarge a space by bouncing light rather than absorbing it, making a room feel more expansive.

DOUBLE UP WITH MIRRORS A well-placed mirror is one of the most cost-effective and easy ways to reflect light and enhance the feeling of space in a small home. For even more light, position a mirror (either a large model or several smaller ones) on a wall across from a glass door or window. Or place a large mirror between two windows to give the impression of a third. Big mirrors can get pricey, but even a few smaller ones within a gallery wall will do the trick.

CHOOSE SHINY FLOORS While carpets can help a space feel cozy and warm, they also consume visual space. Instead, try slightly reflective floors, which bounce light upward and make a room appear larger—especially one with low ceilings. Glossy white floors do a wonderful job of expanding a space, with their light and lofty look, though dark floors can be just as gorgeous and effective (although I'd advise sticking with pale paint on the walls and ceiling). Concrete floors also reflect light nicely, whether they're matte or coated.

014 Master Illusion with Furniture Selection

There's a surprising amount you can do to open up your living room just by picking sofas, tables, and chairs that will work in your favor.

MIND THE SCALE A full-size sectional sofa isn't your best bet in a tiny home. Instead, seek out miniaturized versions of living room staples. Make sure to consider all your pieces in relationship to each other, too: The coffee table should be the same height as your sofa, for instance.

OR GO BIG—REALLY BIG Although it may feel contradictory, sometimes you just have to go with a bigger piece of furniture to truly maximize your space. For example, a tiny sofa with four small chairs might crowd your living room more than one large couch paired with an ottoman. The same principle applies to tabletops. Try not to overburden surfaces with numerous little trinkets—one or two useful statement pieces will make an impact without creating clutter.

ELIMINATE BULK Try finding comfortable furniture that also offers clean lines. An overstuffed armchair can spill visually into the surrounding space, whereas a midsize but well-cushioned slipper chair can provide you with the same comfort without overplaying its role.

LOOK FOR DAINTY FEET When possible, keep the bases of your furniture slender, minimal, and open. Thick table and chair legs crowd floor space, whereas hairpin legs and other streamlined designs allow the eye to take in space around the legs, opening up the room.

OPT FOR TRANSPARENCY Clear glass or acrylic accessories and surfaces keep rooms airy, while opaque items take up visual real estate. (Mirrored furnishings can also lighten up a space.)

015 Nest Tables for a Neat Look

Nesting tables (sets of two or more side tables in ascending sizes) can greatly enhance surface area when you need it—and tuck away, one on top of the other, when you don't. Usually available in lightweight, even delicate materials and shapes, nesting tables are chic and infinitely arrangeable. Put them in a row for a larger coffee table, or distribute them near seating for small-scale, temporary side tables when you have guests.

Another fantastic surface option for modestly sized living rooms is the C-table: a stylish, cantilevered side table that can be placed so it juts over the sides of chairs, sofas, and even beds when you require surface area. When you don't, simply swivel it to the side.

016 Consider Banquette Seating

The couch is always a commitment. As it will likely be one of the two largest items in your tiny home (your bed being the other one), the sofa can't help but be a focal point and set the tone for the rest of your space—and it can't skimp on style or comfort. These days, the home furnishings market abounds with smartly scaled "apartment sofas," which can be up to 18 inches (45 cm) shorter than standard models. But an even more space-savvy option is to go with a built-in solution.

Called banquettes, these custom benches can be installed flush with the wall so you avoid donating crucial inches to a back frame. You can also commission or DIY one in whatever size or shape works for your space—a huge relief if your living room is not only small but also quirky in its dimensions. But perhaps the most satisfying benefit is extra storage: You can design your bench with pullout drawers or a single large compartment for luggage, spare bedding, you name it! Consider a banquette a worthwhile investment, as it can double as dining or office seating when coupled with a folding table, and perhaps as a guest bed when outfitted with linens for your overnight visitors.

017 Embrace Balance

When configuring a tiny multiuse space, it's easy to let all your belongings crowd in wherever they fit. But pleasing configurations are even more crucial in a small home. Try to distribute items of equal visual weight so they balance each other out across the room, bearing in mind that large, dark, colorful, richly textured, or ornate objects can often feel hefty. While symmetrical balance—like you see here between the bookshelves and the sofa and media console—is particularly soothing, you can also create balance asymmetrically by counteracting a heavier piece with a grouping of visually lighter items that takes up a similar amount of real estate. Experiment and see what calms and appeals to your eye.

018 Unify Items in a Vignette

Everyone loves a good vignette: a group of objects arranged artfully that says something about your interests, passions, and experiences. Vignettes can be hard to accommodate when surface area is at a premium, so I recommend sticking to functional yet beautiful objects that you use every day. Regardless, it's important to group them smartly. Choosing objects that are in the same stylistic family and in similar colors and materials will help unify your assortment and reduce visual noise, but try to introduce a little visual variety by presenting different shapes and heights, too. And if you organize pieces on a pretty tray or another dedicated surface, they'll feel like a curated, intentional collection. They'll also be easier to move when you need your furniture to multitask.

019 Keep Windows Airy

Don't obstruct your windows—instead, design to multiply their light! Consider skipping window treatments, if possible, as curtains and blinds tend to bring the walls in and make a room feel smaller, whether those window treatments are drawn closed or thrown open. If you require more privacy, simple, lightweight, and translucent curtains or shades (in a material like linen) will keep the room feeling spacious and bright even when closed off to the outside world. And when open, they can be cinched into clean knots, minimizing how much they encroach on your limited wall space. Try installing tension rods within the window moldings, which will keep your curtains contained and leave your walls wide open.

020 Organize Your Essentials in Baskets

I can't say enough about the value of pretty containers in a small space. They make storage part of the decor, taming clutter while enhancing the room with pleasing texture or detail. Since you can't hide them, highlight them by picking the most beautiful options available. I particularly love using baskets to stash necessities—from pet gear to bags to valet items—and I recommend an assortment in different sizes but similar colors and weaves for a unified look. If this storage can slide under furnishings or onto open shelves, even better.

021 Set Up Zones to Create Order

Small homes may not have walls that partition areas for different functions, but you can still define zones within open floor plans. Outlining distinct areas with different functions will bring a welcome sense of order to a tiny space.

CLAIM A SPACE WITH A RUG The boundaries of a rug prompt us, in our minds, to instinctively see it as a separate room. A small area rug can suggest a foyer where there isn't one or, if the adjacent sitting area is framed by a rug, the lack of floor treatment can also distinguish the entry. Try putting down a long, narrow runner to direct traffic (and your eye) to a more inviting space beyond the front door. When using multiple rugs, keep one neutral, allowing the pattern and color of the neighboring design to shine without creating too much noise in the space.

ENCLOSE WITH FURNITURE Freestanding furnishings that rise up to 30 inches (75 cm) high tend to stop the eye, effectively delineating a zone. In the Cottage, we have a counter-high wall that separates the sitting area and the kitchen, but you could achieve the same effect with a sofa or credenza to divide a conversation area from the kitchen or even the bedroom. This tactic doesn't block light and the view beyond, leaving an impression of a larger space.

OPT FOR OPEN SHELVING If you need a zone divider that also offers storage, add an open shelving unit. Available in materials ranging from wire mesh to hardwood, open-backed bookcases are handy in spaces that need an extra wall; remember that natural light and interior vistas are essential in tiny homes, so choose one that implies separation without blocking illumination. You can then outfit the shelves to be as wide open and airy—or opaque and concealing—as you like. Consider everyday items that would work well on either side of the divider, such as plants, rolled-up blankets, stacks of books, and baskets. By using a recurring element on each shelf, or strategically staggering your functional decor, you can create an arresting visual that looks attractive in the round.

022 Make a Statement with a Room Divider

It's hard to justify large art when wall space is at a premium, so a room divider could be your chance to show off your artistic style. For instance, a modern, understated macramé wall hanging can work as a delicate curtain that both softens and delineates the space. Try it in a traditional folding screen, which provides a more streamlined aesthetic and lets you collapse the screen when it's not in use. Keep it less than 6 feet (1.8 m) high to let air and light in over the top. (You can also stretch macramé taut between the floor and the ceiling using hooks, or go with lighter-weight possibilities, such as fabric panels stretched inside a slim wooden frame.)

If antiques are more your style, look for a beautiful garden gate, distressed mirrored panels, or an old window that can add a strong architectural

element to a simple space. Or, if you want a place to display family photos or children's artwork, fasten your treasures with clips to a rigid wire shelving grid and place it between your zones.

023 Cheat the Built-In Bookshelf Look

Built-in cabinets have a one-of-a-kind look that's hard to beat. (See #162 for how to get this effect in your bedroom.) But here's a sneaky trick: Standard kitchen wall cabinets run 12 inches (30 cm) deep and range from 12 to 15 inches (30–38 cm) wide, which makes them a great off-the-shelf alternative to custom cabinetry. With the doors removed, you have instant open-shelf storage, minimal construction chops required!

Here, the cabinets are oriented sideways and affixed up and over a door frame, which maximizes every bit of wall space. Note that mounting the cabinet boxes high on the wall allows for a nice seating area underneath, and that a coat of cool white paint makes the boxes appear to almost recede back into the wall, contributing to that neat, built-in look.

024 Consider a Mini Makeover

For many of us, altering the physical structure of the space we inhabit isn't possible—either because we rent or due to cost. But if you find yourself with some rainy-day money (and approval from your landlord), consider these simple but game-changing improvements in your main living space.

POCKET THOSE DOORS These magical space-savers open by sliding into the walls rather than swinging out into the room, which has the added benefit of freeing up your walls for storage, too. Check with an experienced builder to see if pocket doors will work in your home, as light switches and load-bearing walls may hinder installation.

LIGHTEN UP WITH FRENCH DOORS Another solution to oversize doors is to replace them with their lightweight French cousins. Whatever the width of your door opening, the space required for a pair of French doors to swing open is half that of a single door—a huge amount of space to get back in your floor plan. When used to connect the exterior, French doors open up the room to the view outside, expanding the space and inviting light that can penetrate other rooms via interior French doors. If you don't have room for French or pocket doors, try an accordion door with inset frosted window panels instead.

RAISE THE CEILING Vaulted ceilings can help a tiny home or apartment feel much bigger than it actually is, so if you're renovating, explore boosting your ceiling above the standard 8-foot (2.4-m) height. Some homes (and homeowners, if you rent) may permit removal of the ceiling entirely, revealing gorgeous, lofty rafters overhead.

BUMP OUT A BAY A bigger investment to consider is building a structural bay that juts out into the yard, borrowing space from the outdoors.

025 Get Your Hands on Natural Textiles

Wicker and rattan, sisal and jute, linen and wool—I love decorating with natural fibers and fabrics that are pleasant to the touch. In addition to being better for you (and the environment) than their synthetic counterparts, these textiles lend a range of detail, from thick basketry to understated nubby braids and lightweight loose weaves to upholstery, rugs, pillows, and drapes. They stand up to regular use, too, developing a lived-in look while remaining durable, and they come in a neutral, easy-to-mix-and-match palette that never goes out of style. I find these textiles especially advantageous in a small space, where every item must pull its weight while contributing to the whole aesthetic and creating comfort.

026 Trade the Coffee Table for a Shelf Behind the Sofa

Coffee tables can really take over your living space. Why not opt for a narrow shelf mounted on the wall behind the sofa instead? It works like a long skinny table, still accommodating the essentials, while opening up your floor plan for foot traffic or an ottoman and immediately making the space appear larger. Plus, the shelf creates a gap behind the sofa—perfect for stashing a folding table or chairs.

STEP ONE Measure the length of your sofa and the height of its back frame. Your shelf should sit about 1 inch (2.5 cm) or so below the top edge of the sofa frame so it almost disappears when viewed from the front. (If you have a sectional sofa with an L-shaped configuration, measure the length of the walls behind both sections.)

STEP TWO Mark the shelf's desired height at intervals on the wall. Then, using a laser level for accuracy, draw a line on the wall to connect the marks. This is where the top of your shelf will sit.

STEP THREE Pick wood for your shelf and decide how deep you want it to be. A svelte 6 inches (15 cm) will provide storage without eating into crucial living space, while 1 foot (30 cm) will allow for magazines and even some coffee-table books. Researching the cost and standard widths of solid wood may figure into your decision— even premium-grade plywood is a good option. Most lumber shops will cut the wood to your measurements.

STEP FOUR Look for an L-shaped bracket, preferably one that accepts flat-head wood screws. Mind the bracket's depth: Ultimately, its horizontal flange should come within 2 inches (5 cm) of the front edge of the shelf. Make sure to use an L-shaped (instead of a triangular) brace, as it will provide clearance for any taller items you may want to store under the table.

STUD

STEP FIVE Measure and mark the board's thickness below the shelf line, then use the level to draw a new line to indicate the bottom of the board. Mark the location of the studs in the wall on this new line, then mark the bracket screw holes at each stud. Mount the brackets to the studs. (Note: With solid wood or plywood, you can leave up to a span of 30 inches/75 cm between brackets before the shelf will sag.)

STEP SIX Put the shelf in place to test its position and stability. If all looks good, remove the shelf and sand and paint both sides before securing it to the bracket. If you want a lamp or other electronics on the shelf, decide where they will sit and drill a half-round hole at the back of the shelf for the cord.

027
Fill Corners All the Way Up

When floor space is at a minimum, bulky cabinetry with swinging doors is not the best option for storage. Instead, scrap conventional furniture and mount a triangular shelf or shelves that meet in a V high in a corner—above any door or window frames, or even the heating unit, as shown here—to organize books, accessories, and mementos. We're lucky that our bedroom has a higher-than-normal ceiling that allows me to display some of the musical instruments that we use regularly (see #075), but even 1 foot (30 cm) extra above a door frame can provide enough space for a similar setup.

For those who have an unobstructed corner, you can install a series of open shelves from floor to ceiling, creating your own modern corner cabinet. Or run a board along the top of a window or door frame for an uninterrupted shelf where you can store all those books you can't part with. Just make sure your setup is sturdy—use the appropriate hardware and secure into studs.

028 Dangle Your Decor

Get creative with vertical storage solutions to literally and figuratively elevate your everyday objects—they'll seem more like beautiful displays and less like utilitarian compromises.

HANG THREE Fruit baskets aren't just for the kitchen. These handy multitiered hanging containers come in a variety of new and vintage styles. Stash remote controls, chargers, little plants, and more in these suspended mesh bowls and get them off your tabletops.

FLOAT INVISIBLE SHELVES Clear acrylic invisible shelves disappear behind plants, books, or baskets, making use of otherwise wasted space. Available online and in container and hardware stores, they can support a surprising amount of weight—some units up to 20 pounds (9 kg).

LIGHT IT FROM ABOVE Floor and table lamps with shades can rob your home of space that's needed for furniture and navigation. Slim, airy pendant lights are visually dynamic and useful alternatives that will draw the eye upward and keep your surfaces uncluttered.

029 Craft a Hanging Magazine Rack

Racks designed to store periodicals consume floor space and push publications out of sight, where they tend to stack up, gather dust, and remain unread. This hanging rack encourages me to explore my magazines because I can actually see them. There's even room to dangle reading glasses right on the rungs. Over the years, I've used this simple, space-saving accessory to display greeting cards, too.

STEP ONE Decide on the number of rungs you'd like on your magazine rack. I went with four, but it's totally up to you. Buy driftwood branches (or forage them yourself, if you live seaside), or cut slender branches of similar lengths from your yard. (For a less rustic look, try simple pine dowels from the hardware store.)

STEP TWO For each rung, drill a small hole—just big enough to slide twine or wire through—about ½ inch (1.25 cm) from both ends.

STEP THREE Paint the ends of your branches a favorite color or wrap them with colorful yarn. Here, I painted each end black and wrapped copper wire around the edge of the paint line.

STEP FOUR Lay the branches out on a table, spacing them to allow enough room for a

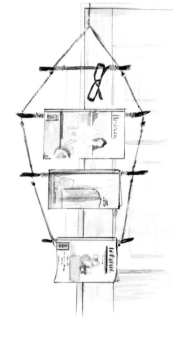

magazine between each. (Most magazines are 8 inches/20 cm wide.) Measure the total distance between the top and bottom branches, then add 24 inches (60 cm). Cut two pieces of twine to that length.

STEP FIVE Thread one twine length through one of the holes in the lowest branch, tying a knot in the bottom end that's bigger than the hole. Repeat with the other length of twine on the other side of the branch. Keep threading the twine through parallel branches, securing with a knot each time.

STEP SIX Pull the two lengths of twine together at the top and tie them in a knot, making a loop with the twine for hanging. Then drape your magazines—covers facing out—over the branches.

While your space may be too tiny for indoor potted trees, you can still liven it up with greenery and florals. In fact, I strongly encourage it, as plants brighten a space, provide texture and detail, and even help purify the air. I'm almost always a fan of the less-is-more mentality, but when it comes to plants, the more the merrier.

030 Press and Frame Flowers

Skip those big, pricey bouquets and go with a floral arrangement you can hang on a wall: a framed assortment of blooms pressed between two panes of glass. It'll last longer than fresh flowers, too.

031 Propagate Clippings in a Beaker

For plant lovers, finding a place to start clippings can be a challenge. Set up your experiments in beakers and other slender, lab-inspired glassware that also make for handsome decor.

032 Cradle Airplants

These tiny, curious plants require zero soil to grow—which means they don't need a pot, which means they take up no space at all! Try dangling them in an artful ceramic display.

033 Try a Plant Stand

Plant stands take up precious floor room. But if you can source sleek, elegant models with skinnier legs that easily tuck into a corner, you'll be able to give a plant or two pride of place on the floor.

034 Hang a Wall Pocket

"Go vertical" is one of my top small-space mantras, but it's especially effective and pretty when it comes to wall-mounted pocket planters. Seek out interesting materials—like galvanized metal or wicker—to display your plants or blossoms, or purchase specially formulated wall-mounted eco planters that allow you to grow a more lush look.

035 "Float" a Plant on an L-Bracket

My readers are always asking how we've hung the trailing pothos plants in our living room, and the answer is so simple it's kind of funny: We affixed white, standard-issue L-brackets high on the wall and just placed the pots on top. This creates an uncluttered and somewhat magical look—as if the plants are hovering just off the wall.

036 String a Garland of Tiny Blooms

This is hands-down my favorite way to display flowers in the Cottage. You can easily source tiny glass bottles online or in a crafts store, then wrap wire around their necks to create a garland. Hang it up wherever you like and rotate in single blooms every week for an always seasonal display. (See #140 for another take on this idea.)

037 Grow Herbs in a Multitiered Hanging Garden

No outdoor space to host your pots of basil, rosemary, and mint? Keep your fresh herbs handy—and off the table—with a hanging planter instead. Some models come with multiple tiers; others you can hook together for a custom solution.

038 Dream Up a Color Palette

For small homes, lighter color schemes often work best, as they create the illusion of more space. That's why I've opted for wall paint and textiles in creamy white throughout the Cottage. This combination bounces light and creates a delightful airiness. I let the foundation of natural wood cabinetry and built-in furniture warm up the pale walls, and I punctuated the look with pops of bright green for a little contrast. If white feels flat in your space (or if you don't have an abundance of natural light), you can get a similar effect with more depth by painting your walls in light beige, gray, or blue.

While this colorway works best for us, you may crave a darker wall color to create a moody and cozy bedroom. Or—if you're a color lover—you may want a boldly painted accent wall as a focal point for your room or even an all-over hue that creates a more jewel-box feel. Follow your instincts, but know that it helps to really pare down to a single color family and an even more limited number of decorative pieces and patterns when you go with dramatic color.

039 Rotate Art and Ornaments

In a small space, it's simply not possible to display all of your favorite things all at once—it would be visually overbearing, and you'd have no place to put down your coffee mug. Instead, embrace the idea of rotating items in and out of storage, between rooms, and from walls to open surfaces. This way, you can create endless new views and vignettes without acquiring new objects, and you'll likely never grow bored of a single corner in your home. (See #018 for more on vignette basics.)

040 Forgo the Frame

When a work of art strikes a chord with you, craft a way to enjoy it daily without spending money on a frame. In addition to adding cost, framed art juts out from the wall, taking up crucial space, and it's arguably harder to part with it when the time naturally comes to let it go. Discover these cash-savvy, space-efficient ways to showcase art instead.

CLIP IT Good old-fashioned binder clips will hold a variety of mixed-media art securely. Add clips of an appropriate size to the top of the piece as well as the bottom, where their weight will steady the paper in a breeze and prevent it from curling over time. Hammer a pair of lightweight nails or tacks into the wall, then slide the clip's handles or holes over them to mount the art.

GO WITH OLD-SCHOOL DOWELS Currently making a comeback as an economical, minimalist way to mount art, hanger frames (reminiscent of vintage educational posters and medical pull-down charts) consist of two wooden dowels with grooves that the poster slides into at the top and bottom. The wood helps define the piece on the wall, but this solution is also lightweight and no trouble to hang, and you can easily swap out the art.

PIN IT Wall pins are a subtle way to mount prints, as they can nearly disappear against the art. For an even more minimal look, try slender T-pins, found in art-supply stores. Conversely, make a statement with push pins in a bold color or style.

041 Pick an Art Strategy

Your walls deserve beautiful artwork, but adorning them in a small space takes a little more thought, as usual. You can go bold with a single vivid painting or print positioned as the focal point of your room, which works brilliantly if your furniture tends to be more minimalist or monochromatic. (Pro tip: If your space lacks a window, displaying a large landscape can feel surprisingly like the real thing.) Or go for the gallery wall, a loose and arty grid of smaller mixed media that can create the illusion of a bigger surface. For welcome negative space, mount smaller pieces onto larger picture mats surrounded by skinny frames.

042
Display with a Swinging Tray

Try showcasing items on a swing shelf—perhaps upcycled from a wooden crate, like mine. A suspended ledge like this is striking yet light and breezy, and you can move it wherever you like with little fuss.

STEP ONE Start with a base. A simple plank of wood will do, or seek out a wooden tray, a handsome cutting board, or even a large terra-cotta tile.

STEP TWO Screw four eyehooks into each corner of your shelf.

STEP THREE Eyeball your space to figure out how high to hang your shelf. Measure this height, double it, and cut two lengths of strong twine to this specification.

STEP FOUR Feed the ends of one twine length through two adjacent eyehooks, creating a triangular loop. Knot off the twine, then repeat with the second length on the other side of the board.

STEP FIVE Suspend your shelf by the center points of both triangles. You can dangle it from a hook or knot both twine loops around a curtain rod or a branch. Deck it out with objects that bring you pleasure—just make sure they're lightweight and not likely to break.

043 Make Up a Spare Bed

When you're entertaining friends over a long weekend, they'll need a place to catch some shut-eye—which is easier said than done when you lack a spare bedroom. The easiest solution is to invest in a sofa that has a trundle, pulls out, or unfolds into a bed. If you've already chosen a nonconvertible couch (or if your space came with a built-in bench, like mine), there are also sleeper chairs that fold out into single beds. (Some pull-out models aren't especially comfortable, so consider adding a mattress topper.) Otherwise, today's air mattresses inflate and deflate quickly, so they're a great option if you can make space for them in your limited floor plan.

Regardless of sleeping surface, endeavor to make the area as welcoming as possible with real bed pillows and linens. It also helps to add a temporary nightstand and light source nearby. The more bedlike you can make it, the more at ease and welcome your guests will feel.

044 Convert Your Living Room for Guests

Don't let a tiny floor plan prevent you from inviting visitors into your little home. Here at the Cottage, we've welcomed guests for stays lasting up to three weeks! If we can do it, I bet you can, too. Here are some helpful tips to keep in mind.

HIDE GUEST BEDDING NEARBY Stash your guest bedding and accessories someplace practical and accessible. A coffee table that doubles as a storage chest is ideal for holding an air mattress and a dedicated set of linens. When the bedding is in use, the chest then becomes a handy storage space for your guests' belongings during their stay.

SCREEN FOR PRIVACY It's obviously challenging to find completely private space for overnight guests in a tiny home, but it's still nice to try. A room divider provides your guests with a little place of their own. If your space can't accommodate a folding screen, try suspending a temporary curtain around the guest bed or couch. In the evenings the curtain creates privacy, while during the day you can cinch it with a decorative pin to leave the room open and airy.

SERVE A CARE PACKAGE When visitors sleep in rooms that fulfill more than one purpose (such as a living room and office that doubles as a guest room, like ours), be sure to offer them eye masks and earplugs. These little things help guests settle in and get a better night's sleep. It's also nice to set up a tray with water, a snack, chargers, your wifi password, and local information.

COLOR CODE GUESTS' TOWELS Use different colors of bath linens, so everyone knows which one is his or hers.

MAKE ROOM IN THE BATH, TOO Temporarily clear a shelf, cubby, or basket in the bathroom for your guests' toiletries. (This is also a great excuse to evaluate your bathroom products and let go of anything you don't need; see #219.) Not only does providing a dedicated space for your visitors' toiletries help them feel welcome, it also prevents clutter from piling up on valuable counter and floor space during their stay.

045 Simplify and Refresh Your Living Space

Let's face it: If you live in a small home, the easiest way to prevent clutter is by regularly surveying your belongings and lightening your load . . . and by preventing anything you don't really need from crossing your threshold to begin with. But from time to time, we all have to do a major overhaul, taking stock of our possessions and considering how much space they take up in our homes and minds. Recycle, donate, or sell the following, and you'll open up ample room for living.

MEDIA Here in the digital age, you can forgo all forms of physical media—from books and magazines to movies and music. While it can be painful to part with these often nostalgic items, if you haven't touched something in three years, it's time to let it go. Dedicate a limited amount of space—say, a single shelving unit—to things you want to keep and then cull ruthlessly, keeping mainly books, magazines, and records that are lovely objects in their own right. Consider any new purchases by the same metric; if it doesn't enhance your space, buy it digitally instead. As for DVDs and CDs, transfer them to your hard drive or the cloud and donate the discs immediately. There is simply no reason to hold on to these relics!

TECHNOLOGY Speaking of relics, clear out obsolete models and duplicates of all your technology: phones, media players, televisions, computers, tablets, and whatever cords and accessories are cluttering up your entertainment area. Most communities have technology-recycling services, and many schools, libraries, and nonprofits accept lightly used gadgets. If you accidentally throw away a cord that you later need, I guarantee that you'll be able to borrow or find one easily.

TOYS AND GAMES Do you have tons of board games but zero actual game nights on your calendar? You know who you are! Whittle down your collection to three or four faves, and find an out-of-the-way space to store them. As for baby toys spilling over into the living space, regularly donate ones that haven't seen play in three months (see #072); for older children, involve them in deciding what to donate. It will help them understand the value of letting go and cultivate the joy of giving.

PAPER Thanks to the miraculous invention of both the portable scanner and shredder (see #058 and #061), I've been able to cut the amount of paper we keep down to just about zero. Another big help has been to go digital when we can. Most banks and credit card companies offer mobile applications that let you photograph and upload receipts via your smartphone, so there's no need to hang on to the original papers. And if you're guilty of leaving yourself sticky notes around your home, try recording reminders on your phone instead. If you find it painful to recycle a beautiful card or artwork from a loved one, keep a single folder for such items and then regularly scan and discard those that no longer pull at your heartstrings.

ITEMS YOU'VE OUTGROWN We have a tendency to accept that, once purchased and installed, an object in our homes is there for good. Over time, you lose the ability to see that, say, your college papasan chair doesn't mix with furniture you bought later on. It's important to look at your space with fresh eyes and let go of pieces that no longer work with the aesthetic or fulfill their intended service. (Does anyone even sit in that papasan chair?) This is especially true if a piece of furniture isn't in great shape; if it's broken or ratty, thank it for its service and responsibly let it go. That goes double for art, decorative objects, and accessories like pillows and throws, as there's no reason to give them space if they don't regularly delight you. Plus, switching them up is an uncomplicated way to refresh a space.

046 Embrace Unexpected Solutions

You don't need to flip through catalogs to find the best furniture for your tiny living room—sometimes, elegant ideas that are just right in size can take you by surprise. For instance, bring in a slim plant stand from the patio for an interesting take on a side table, or make a rolling basket do double duty as cutting board storage when it's not at the farmers' market. Be open to serendipitous fixes, and your space will be all the richer and more personal for it.

We have two rescue beagles, StanLee and Sophee, and I simply can't imagine the Cottage without their sweet antics. I also can't imagine it without their stuff—in a small space, it is impossible to hide! Here's how to make your pet's playthings, food, and other accessories blend in easily with your furnishings and decor.

047 Scale Down the Dog Bed

Dog beds keep getting bigger, but chances are your pooch will find a half-oval or half-circle bed just as comfortable as a full one, and it won't eat up so much of the floor plan.

048 Dangle Leashes by the Door

Keep track of your pup's leash by giving it a dedicated place near the door. If you can, select hooks, leashes, and collars that are suitable for both your pet and your decor.

049 Hang a Scratching Post

If you don't give your cat a surface to scratch, he or she will likely go find one anyway (sorry, sofa). But you can skip the cat tower and go with a wall-mounted scratch board instead. Search for one on Etsy or make your own out of wood and twine. Just make sure to mount it within paws' reach.

050 Set Up a Cat Corner

Cats love getting up above the fray, but a high-rise cat condo is a little much when you barely have room for your own stuff. Mount a small platform in a high corner instead, outfitting it with a small cushion for comfort.

051 Keep a Dedicated Toy Drawer

As much as we love our pets, dog and cat toys can really impact a room's aesthetic—and, when they all get loose, not for the better. We find it helps to keep most of them corralled into a low drawer that our dogs can help themselves to throughout the day.

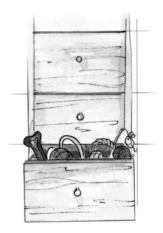

052 Coordinate Food and Water Bowls

Your pet's food and water bowls are a mainstay on the floor, so choose an attractive matching set that you won't mind seeing daily. Likewise, don't even think of having a massive bag of pet food sitting out in plain sight. Pour it into a design-savvy airtight canister, preferably coordinated with your pet's food bowls.

053 Store Grooming Gear in a Roll-Up Pouch

Keep combs, nail clippers, and other pet-care essentials stored together in a compartmentalized pouch that you can roll up and store once the grooming session is over. If you regularly hire a grooming service, consider skipping these items entirely.

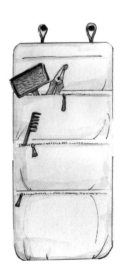

Spotlight

Kim Lewis

054 Meet Kim Lewis of *Extreme Makeover: Home Edition*

You may know Kim Lewis as "the little lady with big ideas," a moniker she earned during her time designing small homes on FYI's *Tiny House Nation* or, before that, her six-year stint as lead designer on ABC's *Extreme Makeover: Home Edition*. "I had spent years of my career designing homes well over 2,500 square feet (230 sq m)," Kim says. "I realized one day while drawing a tiny home: I was finally designing something I could see myself living in!"

Fast-forward, and Kim and her husband Joey have created their own tiny abode in Austin, Texas. Coming in at under 600 square feet (56 sq m), and inspired by Joshua Tree's eclectic desert style, the home's design blurs the boundaries between inside and out, with massive glass doors opening out onto a deck that flanks the home on three sides. It's also not one structure but two: The main living space (with a small home office) shares an open floor plan with a pint-size kitchen, while the bedroom, bathroom, and small laundry nook are found across a breezeway. The couple also DIYed a kitchen island cart on casters that they move around for different uses, and they installed a rainwater collection system for their water supply. If Kim could give one quick tip to anyone building their own tiny home, it'd be to check out the house for storage nooks on high before you close them off with drywall: "Be sure to capture ceiling space when you can! This is where you'll find space for things like luggage, camping gear, and extra blankets."

For Kim, living in a small home facilitates one of her biggest joys: travel. "At the age of 36, I had not bought a home yet because I wanted to have enough disposable income to continue globe-trotting," she recounts. "But with tiny living, I can pay off the home in under three years, and still have enough to see the world." Travel also has the added benefit of helping furnish the couple's space. "Everything in the tiny home has a story. Literally, everything. Curated pieces from around the world, family heirlooms—our entire story is here."

And now, with a baby on the way, Kim and Joey are looking forward to adding another chapter to that story. Does the couple plan on moving into a larger home when the baby arrives? Not a chance. The plan is to simply move the washer and dryer to an outdoor shed, giving their newborn the laundry alcove in their bedroom.

055 Highlight Travel Souvenirs

Have you ever visited someone's home and noticed that the furnishings and decor all come from the same retailer—and from roughly the same catalog, too? When we make a big move, we often rush to set up our homes all at once, as opposed to collecting more meaningful items over time. By contrast, Kim's tiny home is a mini museum of a few well-selected treasures she's discovered in her travels—like an elaborately carved, vivid green headboard that she brought home from Bali for a mere US$100, or a pair of antique antelope busts that she spotted in Africa. Beyond infusing your small space with tons of character, these curios will help your memories live on in your day-to-day mind.

056 Link the Interior with the Exterior

One of the many things I love about Kim's space is its unique relationship with the surrounding landscape. Despite the breezeway separating two distinct structures, the space feels unified by the immense sliding-glass doors in both buildings. Beyond the remarkable view, this approach also makes the outdoors seem like an extension of the interior rooms, with the porch stretching in an L-shape along three sides of the house. It provides ample room for enjoying the vista and lets lots of light in, too, and who doesn't love lying in bed at night and watching the stars? Of course, this tactic isn't for all climates. The warm weather in Austin means that movement between the two structures is usually comfortable. If you live somewhere with mild weather, challenge yourself to find ways to open up your home to the natural beauty right outside your door.

057 Create a Low-Profile Office

Thanks to smartphones and laptops, it's remarkable what we can now go without in a tiny workspace. But there's more involved in creating a flexible miniature home office than modern gadgetry. As you evaluate what you need, don't forget to think of out-of-the-ordinary ways in which you can fulfill those needs. Don't trap yourself within the concept of a traditional office—consider unexpected tools and spaces within your home that can help you accomplish your work beautifully.

I began working from home long before we moved into our little cottage. And, over the years, I've found myself requiring fewer and fewer tangible goods in order to accomplish my jobs. Some of this is due to the world's ever-increasing electronic landscape, but it's also because I've learned what office supplies I can live without—and found hard-working, tiny-space-appropriate versions of the ones that I can't forgo.

PICK A SLIM DESK A desk is nothing more than a table where you can meet your goals—many of us don't need a large surface or tons of drawers or coordinating file cabinets. Look for slimmer models that can also be used as a buffet or a hobby space. Bonus for ones with expansion abilities: My desk has concealed pull-out trays that provide extra inches when needed.

SKIP THE STANDARD OFFICE CHAIR The usual corporate rolling office chair just doesn't fly in our small space; I find that its style, size, and materials make it stick out like a sore thumb. Instead, I've gone with airy stacking chairs that I can turn away from the office area to instantly create extra seating for our living room. For many at-home workers, however, good ergonomics are

not negotiable. If that's you, seek out a low-profile task chair in a color that blends in with your decor. Some even come with more traditional accent materials, such as leather, wood, or brass, which will look nice in a multiuse room.

AUDIT OFFICE SUPPLIES I routinely reevaluate my desk accessories: When was the last time I used a hole punch? Do I really need dozens of pens and pencils? Why on earth do I have white-out and paper clips? Do I still need this stack of heavy instructional books when I search for more current versions of their contents online? Why do I still own a printer when I can visit the local copy shop for my rare print jobs? By getting rid of things I thought I needed—or that I haven't needed in years—I've managed to minimize supplies.

KEEP CLOSE AND CONCEAL My must-haves fit in a slender drawer in my desk, while portable devices I use daily sit out of sight on a small stand behind my computer (see #060). My less frequently used tools occupy zipped pouches that I've stashed in rattan baskets by the couch. This means that I can quickly tuck everything away at the end of each workday, making the living room look and feel like our home rather than my office.

Thanks to our present-day gadgets, you can curate a multiuse workspace that can go from fully functional (and even messy) to tidied up for dinner within minutes. The key? Skipping the standard-size equipment of the past and tuning in to today's compact digital tools instead.

058 Scan Everything

Banish those boxes of receipts, financial records, medical documents, business cards, photos, and more with a compact scanner—some models are no larger than a thick ruler. Once you convert your documents to a digital format, shred the originals if you don't need them and then organize your files electronically. (Be sure to keep a secure backup; external hard drives and cloud storage are smart options.)

059 Hide a Wireless Printer

There's no need to keep a printer on your desk. Even cleverly designed compact models are an eyesore and intrude on the aesthetics of a carefully decorated, multifunctional room. Instead, store a small wireless printer out of sight nearly anywhere (a large drawer or closet shelf would do the trick), and "connect to it wirelessly from all of your devices.

060 Get a Shelf for Your Monitor

While desktop computers are sleeker than ever, their accessories can clutter up a workspace. You can place risers with mini cubbies under your monitor, but they make a mixed-use room feel "office-y." Instead, try securing a shelf to the monitor's back side. This platform can hold an external hard drive, a portable scanner, and USB keys. From their perch, the devices remain plugged in and ready for action, but with their cords out of sight.

061 Shred Paper Right Away

You can shred the occasional paper bill or personal file safely with a hand-operated shredder that's about the size of a pair of sunglasses. If you need to shred a significant number of documents only once or twice a year, take them to an office supply center that offers bulk shredding. There's just no reason to buy and store your own industrial paper shredder.

062 Wrangle Cables

Manage multiple cords with cable sleeves, which corral numerous wires into one bundle that you attach to the underside of a desk. Or, if you're plagued by just one or two cords, keep them in place via small peel-and-stick clips that adhere to nearly any hard surface without damaging its finish. You can also pack your cords out of sight when not in use in a handsome, compact kit that can sit on your desk without detracting from your decor.

063 Take Your Desk with You

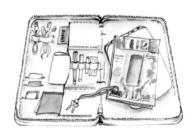

If you use a laptop, challenge yourself to keep your entire office in a stylish portable portfolio. Before investing in one, make sure it offers a handful of key features. Does it hold your charger, wires, earbuds, and earplugs? Will it fit your laptop or tablet? Does it cleanly sort pens, paper, and notepads? Is there a dedicated space for credit cards, an ID, and other items you'll need on the go? Is it beautiful to look at and comfortable to transport?

064 Choose Desktop Accessories in Pretty Materials

Every surface in your home is basically a stage, so carefully consider the objects you display prominently. If an office tool gets a designated spot on your desk, make sure it is as beautiful as can be—perhaps it's made of natural or intriguing materials (like this driftwood business card holder). Handmade and unique details, shapes, or colors can distract from its utilitarian role.

065 Improvise a Desk

The trick to making room for a home office is to change the way you think about workspaces. Let go of the idea of a dedicated desk and a file cabinet, and you'll begin to see practical, versatile places for getting the job done.

DOUBLE UP Seek multifunctional furniture that can transform from a daytime desk to a dining table in the evenings, or a slim console that can share desk and entryway duties.

FOLD OUT A SECRETARY There are several wall-mounted desks on today's market that you can fold out into a work surface at 9 a.m. and fold back up flush against the wall at 6 p.m. Some of these fit into a simple small box on the wall; many come with built-in organizational cubbies, too.

MAKE IT TO STOW A collapsible half-circle table can easily hold a laptop and office tools when needed. When your work for the day is complete, fold and slide it under a bed or behind a couch.

RIG IT UP Another option is to craft your own solution, like the DIY midcentury-modern-inspired system of floating shelves at left with a small desk nestled in among plants and decor. While it reads designer, it's just shelf tracks, brackets, and boards.

066 Put Unexpected Nooks to Work

If you're struggling to find an unused corner for a desk, consider passageways such as the foot of the bed, staircase landings, and even hallways. These spots are out-of-the-ordinary choices, but they just might be all the room you need. For example, when we need a second office at home, I set up a folding table on our back stoop. I hang a curtain temporarily on a pole across the partially open doors to block the wind and keep things a bit warmer—it works just fine and looks lovely.

067 Cleverly Stash Office Supplies

You don't need bulky filing cabinets, bookshelves, or even desk drawers to keep your workspace tidy and accessible. Suss out the items that you truly use, and donate the ones you don't. From there, look for creative ways to organize your necessities.

PUT IT ON ROLLERS A rolling shelf set (such as one of those on-trend multiuse bar carts; see #072) can be the perfect solution for storing your books, paperwork, and accessories, keeping them as close as needed without having to dedicate a spot for them in your living area. When the workday is done, roll the cart out of sight.

ZIP UP STUFF IN PLAIN SIGHT If you have shelving available, use zipper pouches to contain and beautify your office supplies and small electronics, then store them in baskets.

THINK OUTSIDE THE FILE BOX In a small space where everything is visible, nothing is worse than a plastic or metal filing cabinet. It's not just ugly, it's a constant reminder of work. Instead, repurpose containers like rustic picnic baskets or travel gear. Whether you prefer to shop handmade, vintage, or designer brands, there's no shortage of beautiful travel bags and briefcases that can serve as your mini office on a daily basis.

068 Audition Tiny Speakers

Sound travels well through a small space. As such, most tiny homes need only a decent Bluetooth speaker paired to a computer or mobile device for quality ambient sound. But if you're an audiophile and desire a professional sound system in your small space, invest in inset speakers (either in-ceiling or in-wall), which will invisibly elevate your sound and leave your surfaces clear for other items.

069 Ditch the TV—or Mask It Well

Before bringing a TV into your small living space, ask yourself: Can I watch shows and movies happily on my computer? If so, skip it. But if you want a big screen, here's how to cope with it in a small space.

CAMOUFLAGE IT Try finding artistic ways to conceal your TV amid other decor, such as making it recede into a gallery wall or a collection staged behind it. It's also easy to quickly cover a wall-mounted TV with a tapestry or even an artfully mounted rug on the wall.

ROLL IT AWAY If your monitor is small, consider keeping it and any accessories on a rolling cart, which you can stash in the closet when not in use.

INVEST IN GOOD TECH There are an increasing number of design-savvy TVs on the market that come in slim frames and display digital art of your choosing when not in streaming mode. They're a beautiful solution, and you can change the art with just a few clicks.

070 Go Big Screen with a Projector

If you just have to have a big-screen image but don't want to donate space to the traditional 120-inch (3-m) TV, a projector may make more sense. The projector itself is small and lightweight, and it streams content from your laptop or desktop computer. You can mount it to the ceiling with simple hardware, or it can live on a bookshelf or mantel. (We keep ours on a rolling cart and rig it higher when needed.)

You'll still need a big screen, but try rolling it up and mounting it to the ceiling or recessing it so it's out of the way. If it annoys you to have to manually raise and lower the screen, opt for one that has a remote control. At the Cottage, we also like to watch movies in our back garden, so we store a collapsible screen vertically in a closet corner and quickly pop it up when desired.

Just as TVs range widely in price, so do projectors and screens, but these days you can actually buy a front projection setup for a lot less than a big-screen TV. Just remember: The darker the viewing space, the better you'll be able to see the screen.

071 Hide Your TV in a Pretty Display

Putting a big black TV front and center can make a small space feel dark, cramped, and too techy. While I suggest mounting a projector and/or streaming your media on a computer (see #069 and #070), you can also conceal a TV when it's not in use. Try this cabinet with folding doors—its simple picture frames encase botanical prints, the perfect disguise for the electronics inside.

STEP ONE Measure your TV's height, width, and depth, as well as the depth of a fixed TV wall mount, to arrive at your cabinet's rough dimensions. The cabinet should look centered, but it's critical that it span at least two studs. You may need to make it wider to accommodate stud placement and still look centered when closed.

STEP TWO Choose botanical prints and picture frames to fit. I adore wood, but a subtle decorative metal would also be lovely. Measure the frames and make any adjustments to your initial cabinet size so you can accommodate eight frames total, arranged two per cabinet door. Sand, paint, or stain the frames now, if desired.

STEP THREE Place your frames on ½-inch (1.25-cm) plywood and use their height and width as a guide to cut four narrow, equal-size doors. When laid out side by side, the doors will make up the front of the cabinet.

STEP FOUR Using spray adhesive, adhere your prints to each piece of plywood, then glue the frames on top. Once dry, secure with finishing nails through the back of the plywood.

STEP FIVE Attach a pair of bifold hinges to the backs of two doors. Repeat with the other two doors. Lay the doors side by side on a flat surface and measure them to arrive at the precise size of the cabinet's frame.

STEP SIX Assemble the cabinet frame with wood glue and nails, then use bifold hinges to attach the doors to the frame. Cut two 1x2 boards long enough to span the cabinet's interior. With wood glue and wood screws, attach one each to the frame's top and bottom.

STEP SEVEN Hold the cabinet in place, check the level, and mark its future spot. Drill wood screws through the mounting boards at each stud to support the cabinet. Attach the TV wall mount to the studs with wood screws, then attach your TV.

STEP EIGHT Apply plywood veneer strips to the raw edges, and sand, seal, or paint. Add a knob or handle to the front-facing board so you can pull it out with ease.

072 Set Up a Play-by-Day Station

It's so important to me that my sweet boy has a safe, interactive, and exciting area to play during his waking hours—but it's also important that my husband and I have a less chaotic adult space in the evenings. So for us, it works best to take five to ten minutes each morning to set up a dedicated space with a play pad and toys.

START FROM THE GROUND UP A clean, cushioned pad, as large as is practical, is the first step in creating a daily play space for young family members. Whether setting up inside or out, pick one that rolls or folds down to a compact size that you can easily stow. Many have designs on both sides for a colorful, washable, visually stimulating surface on which your child can play.

TOTE THE TOYS If you already store children's books and toys in bins and baskets, it's simple to ferry them to the pad. If those items live in built-in shelving or permanent storage containers, select some pieces that your child will enjoy and use a rolling market basket or bar cart to carry and contain the items throughout the day. Depending on their age, your children can help you with this— it can be a fun activity in itself.

INSPECT DAILY At the end of the day, as you're stowing everything away, take the time to remove the toys and tools that are wearing out or that your child is outgrowing. You'll be amazed at how simple it is to maintain a steady balance of incoming and outgoing children's items this way. When you do it in real time, you feel less sentimental about discarding things because you're making room for the next stage in your child's development—which is a greater cause for joy than holding on to every souvenir.

073 Grow the Play Space

As your child grows, you'll likely find yourself needing more room. Be clever when considering how to find new space within the confines of your home. What areas border the daily play space? An office? If so, perhaps you can convert your desk into a wall-mounted standing model, freeing up floor space. In the bedroom, try to eliminate nonessential furnishings that sit on the floor by relocating their contents to vertical storage. Or perhaps it's the kitchen. If so, roll your bar cart or island temporarily to another area, opening up additional inches for play.

074 Seek Out Beautiful Toys

One frequent complaint from parents everywhere—regardless of the size of their homes—is the unattractiveness of many children's toys. Often made of bright-colored plastic, many toys are magnets for the eye in a tiny space. Since any object in your home needs to function as decor, be very choosy with any toys you buy and bring home; look for books with delightful covers and charming blocks and dolls in wood or other natural materials. (Bonus points for buying handcrafted pieces from artisans instead of big-box stores.) Stimulate your child's development by introducing them to colors and patterns, but try stowing the visually noisier designs when your little one is done with them. Of course, always be mindful of safety when shopping for babies, steering clear of easily swallowed or otherwise dangerous items.

075 Show Off a Passion

The evidence of some hobbies can be hard to hide—and some instruments, gear, and apparel are so beautiful, why would you want to? I personally love seeing tools of the trade (whether for sports, music, or art) given pride of place in a home. And if the enthusiast in question is school-age, selectively exhibiting their supplies is a great way to celebrate their achievements.

GET ON BOARD So many skateboards and surfboards are beautifully designed and crafted, so be sure to show them off! Mount a surfboard on a large wall or overhead for a striking yet graceful piece of statement art (and quick access whenever the waves come in). Likewise, you can hang a boldly decorated skateboard on the end wall of a bookcase or a narrow wall space, or arrange a collection of boards on invisible floating shelves.

SHOWCASE A MUSICAL INSTRUMENT Whether they're strings or keys, bass or drums, musical instruments tend to make wonderful decor, thanks to their dramatic shapes and rich materials. Again, displaying instruments as wall art is better than hiding them away. If you have several, arrange them in a row from smallest to largest; or mount a single instrument in an arrangement of vintage album covers or framed antique sheet music for a thematic display.

HIGHLIGHT ART SUPPLIES Our homes should be havens for our creative sides, and while small-space dwellers can rarely spare surfaces for elaborate or sizable painting projects, a tray containing an edited vignette of beautiful brushes or palettes—or knitting needles and yarn, whatever your passion—will hopefully inspire you to do what you love more often. Pair them with inspirational images or objects currently feeding your creativity.

076 Stash Your Sports Gear

For fitness fans, workout equipment must be convenient to access (even more so for those who need a prompt to get going). But when you live in a small space, you certainly don't have a home gym, spare closet, or laundry room in which to store your gear. Plus, the different sizes and formats make it a challenge to lump them all into one category. (For instance, the way you stash your basketball won't be the way you store your yoga mat or tennis racket.) It's easiest to look at each piece separately and craft solutions according to its shape and dimensions.

HANG YOUR MAT There are so many yoga mat racks and containers on the market—and each one is more unnecessary than the last. Just fasten a strap around your mat and suspend it over a hook on the inside of a closet door (or on a wall, if you really love your mat's design).

STORE STRENGTH-TRAINING TOOLS Bands, rings, ropes, and free weights don't take up much space themselves, but they quickly clutter a space when left out in the open. Keep these workout essentials hidden within a basket or bin, or string the lighter ones up to prevent tangles.

ROUND UP BALLS AND BATS Large spherical items do present storage difficulties, which are often exacerbated by their bright colors or loud patterns. Try corralling balls in a canvas laundry sack and hanging them in a closet, or string bungee cords between two wall-mounted rails and slide the balls behind them. As for rackets or bats, arrange them in a graphic display over a doorway or on the back of a door itself. If they aren't handsome, conceal instead: Stash them behind a row of bins or in an attractive umbrella stand.

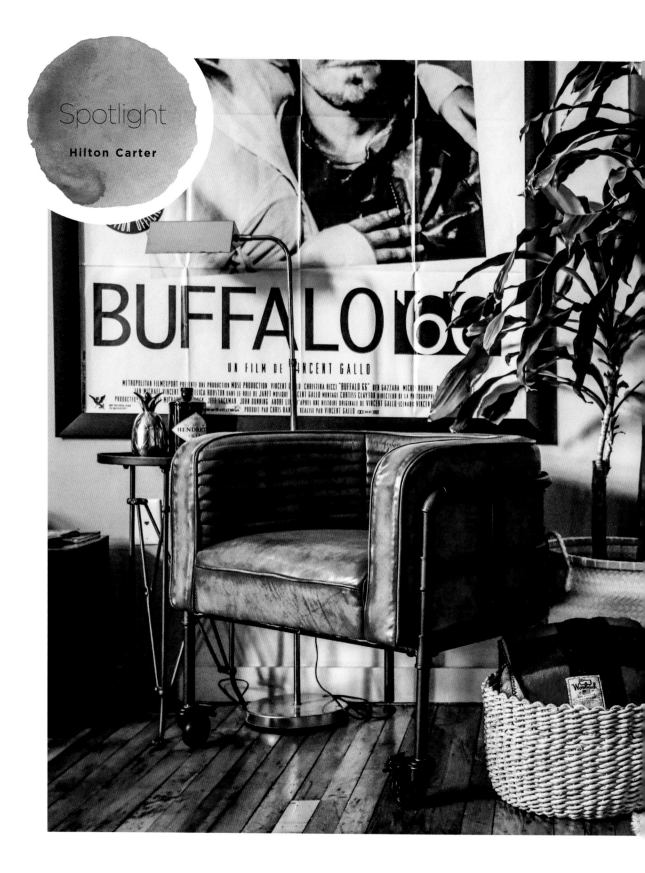

077 Meet Hilton Carter

If you've pinned or liked a photograph of verdant plants online recently, there's a pretty good chance it was taken by the incredibly talented designer, filmmaker, and ultimate green thumbsman Hilton Carter. "I have a personal need to live half in a greenhouse and half in a normal apartment," Hilton says. To achieve that goal, he's made about 180 plants thrive in the 850-square-foot (80-sq-m) home that he shares with his wife Fiona in Baltimore, crafting an aesthetic that's industrial but with romantic old-world touches and a big dose of tropical abundance, too.

Hilton cultivated his love of plants when he was living in New Orleans, where he wanted to bring the city's lush foliage inside. He started with a fiddle-leaf fig plant, then a snake plant, then a rubber tree plant. "If you had set up a time lapse, you'd have seen plants pop up until the room was covered," he says. When he headed back to his hometown of Baltimore, the greenhouse came along.

Hilton's apartment may have a small footprint, but its architecture is epic and open. The space has immense ceilings, ranging from 12 to 24 feet (3.5–7.3 m), and massive windows that let in tons of light—which further opens up the space vertically and also helps his plants thrive. With their warm, worn floors and weathered surfaces, the rooms are rich with texture, contrast, and visual interest: "'Patina' is my favorite word," Hilton laughs. "You need it to bring that edge to a space."

Furniture scale and fit is important to any room, but when you plan on using it to warehouse a nursery, it's even more crucial. Hilton's advice is simple on this front: Purchase for your current space—not your someday house—and sell or donate anything that doesn't work for it. "Skip the insanely large couch," he counsels. "Don't cram all the furniture up against the wall—instead, open it up and create flow."

While Hilton credits his lack of sentimentality to moving around in his twenties, his background in filmmaking also plays an undisputed role: His home is a set, and what doesn't aid the story doesn't make the cut. "The space has to tell you about the character," he explains. He's art-directed his home so that visitors get not just a sweeping pan of what's generally important to him but they can also zoom in on more specific details. "Just like my plants, my framed Dr. Dre *The Chronic* album adds to the story of who I am," he says. "They may not notice it the first time they come over, but more and more, guests learn about me through little displays like that."

078 Stagger a Collection

Collections are a great way to showcase your passions, but making room for multiples in a small house can be tricky—especially if your collection of choice takes up a coveted floor or table surface. Hilton's advice for making it all feel deliberate and airy? Stagger and layer. "I'm 6 foot, 5 inches (1.9 m)," Hilton says. "So I know in a group photo I've got to stay in the back. Nobody ever sees my shoes."

It's the same with your plants or other collections of varying scales: Arrange them so the largest items are distributed toward the rear, then layer medium-size items throughout the midground, and fill out the foreground with smaller, more detailed items. Remember to space them intentionally, clustering items in uneven numbers and providing enough negative space that light can penetrate and the plant can peek through.

079 Go Organic with Your Decor

At the Cottage, I'm always trying to swap out decorative items that will last for hundreds or thousands of years with organic ones that will naturally and gently decay once their time is up. This includes greenery, but also blooms and natural finds like driftwood, stone, and sea glass. Hilton is a master at this, skipping tchotchkes and merely ornamental objects almost completely in favor of heaps of houseplants. Each plant has its own thing going for it—smooth or spiky, voluminous or slender, deep-dark green or variegated in color—while still contributing to an overall harmony. Consider their vessels, too, as these accessories provide you with an opportunity to slip in some extra style. Hilton mixes it up with ceramics, poured concrete, metallics, and glass beakers, in addition to more traditional terra-cotta pots.

080 Highlight Your Ride

Bike storage is a big deal in small urban apartments. It makes perfect sense to keep your wheels indoors, but avoid rolling them through your living space, tracking in all the gifts of city life. You can get your bike out of the way by mounting it to your wall with a store-bought bike shelf (as shown above), or even DIY a sturdy solution: a plaque outfitted with ladder J-hooks, a reinforced shelf made of two planks with a gap left between them for the crossbar, or something more high-end. There are also ceiling-mounted pulley systems that allow you to lift your bike out of the way without overexerting yourself.

081 Go High and Narrow in a Hallway

During my years in Manhattan, I lived in a beautiful, teeny-tiny one-bedroom apartment. It had a narrow and almost comically long entrance hall that made up at least one-fourth of the entire unit. Rather than wasting the square footage, a previous tenant had created brilliant storage solutions along the ceiling of the hallway, which inspired me to add a few more of my own. Here are some handy takeaways—cherry-pick the ones that work for you.

MOUNT HIGH SHELVES Even with standard-height ceilings, you can usually find room along the upper walls of the hall. Install overhead shelves or open shelving cubes across the width of your hall several feet apart to accommodate a library or a system of bins and baskets.

LINE IT WITH CABINETS For a more polished and concealed look, try mounting a row of cabinets to the ceiling that extends the full length of the hallway. Hang a folding step stool nearby for instant access.

HEAP ON THE HOOKS Installing screw hooks along the edge of the bottom of your wall-mounted cabinetry will also instantly create a place to hang jackets, handbags and grocery sacks, aprons, dog leashes, decor—you name it. You could also mount a clothing rail to the underside of the shelves, then suspend S-hooks and hangers for your belongings.

082 Organize a Hallway with Slim Furnishings

A full-size credenza is likely too big for a hallway in a smaller home. Instead, search for shallow storage solutions (about 6 inches/15 cm deep) and surfaces that won't jut out too far into the thoroughfare, impeding through traffic. Try narrow, wall-mounted foldaway drawers designed specifically for shoes but that you can repurpose in myriad ways; skinny, half-width console tables to hold catchalls and decor; and lean lockers for children's toys. If space is really just too limited for a floor solution, go with a simple picture ledge, which can span the whole length of a hallway and provide both storage and display, in a scant 3 inches (7.5 cm) from the wall.

083 Line Up Step Baskets

A staircase eats up a big chunk of real estate. But you can remedy the problem with innovative storage options. Try placing step baskets—clever tiered containers that straddle two steps—along your staircase. Use one to stash miscellaneous items that you often need on your way out, such as leashes, compact umbrellas, and reusable shopping bags. Or queue up several to create storage solutions for everything from craft supplies to guest linens. (Of course, regular baskets will do just fine—look for ones the width of your steps.)

084 Go for Custom Under-Stair Storage

The possibilities for using the open space beneath the stairs are almost limitless. With most of these projects, you'll need to talk with an experienced carpenter about how to modify the space while maintaining structural support for the staircase.

INSTALL PULL-OUT CABINETS Whether you need a solution for your wardrobe or a full bar, custom-built pull-out cabinets are remarkably efficient, utilizing every bit of that under-stair void. (See #126 for a similar idea in the kitchen.)

BUILD IN A PURPOSEFUL NOOK At the higher end, you can install a small home office, a mudroom with a built-in bench, or a stacked washer-dryer combo under the stairs.

HIDE STUFF IN DRAWERS You can also ask a carpenter to help you fill the space with drawers of all sizes, starting with deep ones on the bottom and getting smaller toward the top. Think through the categories of items you plan to store there to decide on the depth and configuration of drawers.

FAKE IT A less expensive approach is to simply line up a few freestanding bookshelves or cabinets in ascending heights so they fit under the sloping stairs. To kit out cabinets, mount sliding drawers and shelves inside them; for bookshelves, simply display your favorite reads or mementos, or slide in matching baskets for a harmonious system of catchalls.

ADD A TRAP DOOR Do you have a landing that's too small to convert to an office or a crafting nook, but big enough that it's consuming coveted square footage? Perhaps you can modify it with stealthy lift-top storage. With the help of a hinged trap door—which doubles as the landing surface itself—you could potentially have a space that's large enough to hold as much as a standard trunk.

CONCEAL DRAWERS IN THE STAIRS Another great option for custom carpentry is to open up the toekick of each stair and turn it into a drawer with a notched finger scoop. It's especially useful for shoe storage near the entryway.

085 Set Up a Mini Garden Getaway

Even the tiniest slice of earth outside your home—a stoop, a driveway, an alley, a porch, or a little garden—can be transformed into a useful, tranquil retreat with minimal effort and cost. Indeed, encompassing any outdoor areas is a delightful and effective way to enlarge and enhance your living space. Tailor your outdoor oasis to your style and taste, but keep your climate in mind when selecting plants, furnishings, and decor.

We are so lucky we can enjoy being outside almost year-round, thanks to the Southern California climate. Plus, the size of our living space nearly doubles when we make use of the outdoors. (Even with our yard and porch taken into account, we still live in under 800 square feet/75 sq m.) The Cottage's outdoor area stretches around three sides of the home, and each side presents many possible outdoor "rooms." We constantly reinvent these spaces to suit our daily needs.

ENTERTAIN ON THE FRONT PORCH We share a 20-by-8-foot (6-by-2.4-m) platform with the neighboring home at the front of the Cottage. We access it through a Dutch door in our kitchen, and it serves as an herb garden, a dining room, a living room, a screening room (we just set up a projector when we want to watch a movie), a playroom, and a bar. We have a simple and lovely lattice garden (see #093) and an outdoor storage bench used as a couch. We set up a table and chairs for guests when we have larger parties.

COME AND GO VIA THE SIDE YARD The front porch steps down into the side yard,

a corridor that connects our home and the neighboring house to a shared laundry and bike shed. This green corridor is much more than a thoroughfare, though: It becomes a more private dining room (sometimes with floor cushions, sometimes with tables), an activity center for our son, a seedling incubator, and an additional office space when we need it. It also is the main point of entrance for the Cottage itself, as the front stoop leads up from the side yard into our living room. This stoop is always tremendously helpful as a solo seating area and a storage space for our market baskets (see #001).

RETREAT TO THE BACK GARDEN For precious family time, we look no further than the private garden (shown at right) and patio behind our cottage. Accessed via the side yard or the French doors that open from our bedroom, it is practically an extension of our interiors. Beyond being peaceful and richly covered in various vines, it also contains our outdoor wardrobe and gardening supplies. The back stoop is frequently an extra workspace, a reading nook, and an outdoor bathing space for our son.

086 Take Your Patio from Cramped to Cozy

If you're fortunate enough to have even the smallest outdoor area, you simply can't miss the chance to make it into a functional yet dreamy retreat. Here are some of my tips for opening and livening up a tiny patio.

LAY DOWN A RUG Indoor-outdoor rugs are one of the easiest ways to define a patio area while adding style and comfort. Available in myriad sizes, prints, and textures, these snappy mats can instantly upgrade your outdoor space; plus, patterns underfoot tend to break up the area, creating the illusion of increased square footage. For an even more on-trend look, mix and match, layer, and stagger more than one rug in the space. If you've never encountered one, an indoor-outdoor rug lets water run through the weave and is specially designed to stand up to the sun without fading. Most are simple to maintain, but always check the tag for care instructions.

SET THE MOOD Lighting is the best way to add a magical touch to your outdoor living space—plus, it will really encourage you to make the most of it in the evening, especially during warmer months. Outfit café strands with warm bulbs and mix them with hanging and floor lanterns for a varied glow.

PROBLEM-SOLVE WITH PLANTS If you're contending with an ugly stretch of exterior wall or an awkward utility box, look for a potted or hanging plant. Trailing vines such as ivy or bougainvillea can also conceal just about anything, while scented wonders like jasmine smell as heavenly as they look.

LOAD ON THE DECOR If your tiny porch, balcony, or corridor has walls, treat them as you would an interior wall. Hang unbreakable acrylic mirrors to visually enlarge the space, as well as outdoor serving trays, plants, or a bucket of votive candles, ready to light. Salvage resilient decor pieces—like driftwood, river stones, or terra-cotta or galvanized steel vessels—and style them into dramatic focal-point displays or detailed vignettes.

087 Turn Storage into Seating

Place sturdy patio storage benches and trunks against an exterior wall, add outdoor seat cushions, and take a seat—it's just that simple! The storage bins can conceal landscaping tools, cleaning supplies, or even luggage. (Do protect any indoor items in moisture-proof bags.) You can toss on a throw pillow or two to support and cushion your back, or go one step further and hang cushions along the wall for a faux sofa back: Mount a drapery rod to the wall—after testing to make sure guests won't bump their heads against it,

of course—and stitch fabric ties to the cushion corners so you can secure them to the rod. (You can also look for storage benches with built-in back rests, like you see here.) Be sure to keep plenty of throws handy for chillier nights, or just for cozying up during outdoor movie night.

088 Keep Patio Furnishings Flexible

A table that folds up completely is a wise choice for tiny stoops and balconies that host many different activities. Even in an itty-bitty area, a semicircular table can seat two people, and the rounded corners eat up less space (both visually and physically) than a comparable square. Rely on hangable folding chairs, which can also be used indoors for pop-up dining or at a desk.

089 Establish and Enjoy Communal Zones

Tiny house living sometimes involves sharing with your community—for instance, at the Cottage, we share our washer and dryer and our porch with the neighboring bungalow. While we've outfitted the 8-foot (2.4-m) width of our deck with decor that we find practical and beautiful, we make sure to keep our neighbors in the know when we need to make changes to the space or plan on having guests over. We also refrain from using it late at night or early in the morning, since sound travels easily through such close quarters. If you share space, it's always helpful (and more enjoyable) to establish open communication, do your part in the upkeep, and respect noise levels and privacy.

090 Get the Jungle Look

'I receive so many comments and questions about our back garden. It's such a refuge for our small family—we're able to use it as a place to gather for relaxation, play, entertaining, and work. A big part of its appeal is all the leafiness, which—in addition to being charming—helps create a private, cozy space and provides shade under the Southern California sun. Of course, your climate will drive what plants you choose for your own backyard. The majority of our greenery is fast-growing trumpet vines, easy-to-manage succulents, and unfussy ficus trees. If you're the type of person who is constantly reconfiguring your space, try a potted garden, which allows you to tweak your plant placement to best suit both seasonal sunlight and your decor. Want to settle in for the long haul and focus on covering up outdoor hardware? Try year-round vines and canopying trees that will thrive in the native environment.

091 Create Privacy with Greenery

Most small outdoor areas lack privacy. From split balconies that overlook facing apartments to stoops that lead to shared sidewalks and gates, it can be tricky to maintain light and airflow while simultaneously attaining a feeling of seclusion. This issue can be particularly challenging for renters and for those operating on a tight budget. Luckily, there are some delightful work-arounds.

BUY A PRIVACY SCREEN If you have an aversion to DIY projects, there are out-of-the-box options available, such as patio privacy screens (with or without planters included). Most of these fold up into compact sizes, and many can be customized to include the number of panels to best suit your needs. You can also try full-length drapes made of outdoor fabric, which can also soften the look of railings, concrete, and other hard exterior surfaces. Ready-made panels are widely available in solid hues and fashionable patterns.

EXPAND A WILLOW TRELLIS It doesn't get much easier than the willow trellis, an adjustable, accordion-style barrier sold in home-supply centers. Mount or suspend one or more in your outdoor nook, customizing its width to suit your space, and plant your favorite trailing vines.

GROW A GUTTER GARDEN Multitiered gutter gardens are a wonderful way to introduce greenery while creating a visual barrier between your home and the rest of the world. You can use chain lengths to suspend three stacked gutters from a sound structural beam, then plant quick-growing vines (such as ivy) for a lush screen effect. Or, if you already have a fence and would like to soften it with greenery and flowers, simply mount your gutters between two of the fence's supports and grow herbs or pretty blooms. Some garden shops and nurseries also offer ready-made versions of this attractive small-space solution.

092 Put a Tiny Balcony to Good Use

Don't overlook the potential of a small balcony! Even if there's barely room for a chair, and the view is of your apartment building's parking lot, you can still make some magic happen.

STACK YOUR GARDEN It always helps to get a little greenery right outside your door, and even more so if you live in a city. But you don't have to choose between a small chair and a plant collection. If you pile up a vertical array in thematic pots (textured baskets help in a spare space), you'll likely also have room for a folding chair or two.

MAXIMIZE THE RAILING If your sliver of space has railings, don't think of them as barriers—think of them as bonuses. Planters designed especially for balcony railings are long and slender and have a mechanism to secure them to the outside of the railing—an easy way to beautify the space and privatize your little sanctuary. Put the railings to work even harder by having a professional affix a bar counter to the top, instantly providing you with a permanent place to dine and work. It could be as narrow as 1 foot (30 cm) and still offer useful surface space. (There are also ready-made versions of these tables available; just keep safety in mind when installing, and make sure that items can't accidentally slide off the surface.)

DIY

093 Hook Your Plants to a Lattice

Living walls are great for small patios without ground area for potted plants or garden patches. I adapted the idea to a more manageable scale with a lattice garden, which offers privacy while enhancing the lounge area at one end of our porch. You can make your own in a weekend and enjoy it through the seasons—just swap out plants as the months roll by.

STEP ONE Measure your space. Standard-issue 8-by-4-foot (2.4-by-1.2-m) panels of lattice are available at big-box hardware stores, so figure out in advance how many you'll need. (You can also take your measurements with you and have the lattice cut to size in the store.) We fixed our lattice to an existing fence, but you could also mount it to 4x4 posts (one for every 4 feet/1.2 m of lattice); just be sure to install them safely and securely in the ground.

STEP TWO With wood screws and a drill, secure the lattice panels, edge to edge, to the fence posts, screwing in every 3 feet (1 m) to make it for keeps. Before you begin attaching plants, seal or paint the lattice. I went with a soft white to keep the space feeling open and bright.

STEP THREE For visual variety, choose a mix of lightweight pots and longer balcony planters, then paint them to match the lattice. (Keeping things monochromatic will create the illusion of a larger space.) It helps to select pots with a lip by which you can hook them to the lattice. Whatever you go with, make sure they have holes for proper drainage.

STEP FOUR Use multiple S-hooks—also available at hardware stores—to hold the pots and planters on the lattice and make it easy to swap them out. If you'd like to hang your pots permanently, attach them to the lattice with screws.

EATING

Sharing a meal is one of life's great joys. Make the most of these moments with a dining setup that is elegant, effortless, and perfectly tailored to your tiny space.

094 Create a Compact Yet Comfortable Kitchen

Kitchens are the hardest-working spaces in any home. They're where we make and enjoy meals, of course, but they also often serve as gathering places, spots for work or craft projects, and thoroughfares in and out of the home. Despite these many roles, there's no reason you can't survive—and even thrive—with a tiny kitchen.

Our mini galley-style kitchen is so much more than a place for cooking and eating, thanks to its open surfaces and mix of exposed and enclosed storage.

CLEAR A SPACE FOR FOOD PREP We're lucky to have decent countertop space for a small home, but we still make efforts to open up surfaces for chopping and cooking. We're able to accommodate smaller appliances (such as a water carbonator, a mini toaster, and a single-serving blender) out in the open, but more often than not, we stash those items in pullout drawers in our base cabinets.

SEEK OUT SMALL APPLIANCES Surprise: Kitchen appliances aren't one size fits all. Dig deeper when seeking refrigerators, stoves, and dishwashers. Compact, counter-depth models are available in a variety of heights and widths. (No space for a range hood? Try an under-cabinet design, or a ventilation fan instead.) We also have a 15-inch (38-cm) sink—which is about half the size of those found in most kitchens—and we opted for a streamlined pullout faucet. Unless you are a professional cook, feed a big crew every day, or store tons of food in the freezer, you don't need full-size appliances. Search for so-called apartment versions and gain precious inches of space.

MAXIMIZE STORAGE Our kitchen cabinets hold food products, cleaning items, and washable wraps, bags, and linens. We use stackable and nesting kitchenware, which preserve a surprising amount of space within our drawers and cabinets. We also display our prettier pieces, including our everyday plates and mugs, in open storage (see #107 for more on open shelving) and prop or hang our best wooden cutting boards as reminders that the utilitarian can be beautiful.

CARVE ROOM FOR MEALS Our breakfast counter is just the right size for a family of three. We found counter stools with backs, so they're comfortable for more than a few minutes at a time, and we have enough room between them for West's high chair, which can convert into a counter-height or dining-height chair as he grows. The first third of the counter is left bare, ready for us to unload groceries, open the mail, cut greenery, and so forth. The middle third is reserved for dining or working. And the last third, which backs up to the Dutch door, is where we prepare tea and coffee every morning, and where we keep a tray or basket of food-safe wipes for quick cleaning.

095 Use Large Appliances for Storage

Tiny kitchens can be every bit as practical and usable as their more spacious counterparts with the help of some innovative thinking. Look to your larger appliances in particular, which can take on double-duty roles in a way that not only facilitates cooking and cleaning but also enhances the character of your little home.

STORE IN AND ON THE OVEN When not in use, your oven can house cookware and larger platters. (If you do embrace this storage tactic, never turn it on without first checking inside!) I find it helps to keep the coffee carafe, teapot, and saucepan on the stovetop all the time, even when I'm not using them—just select practical yet stylish designs since they're always in sight. Treating these mainstays as decor frees up storage space and gives your kitchen a welcoming, personal feel.

LOAD UP THE FRIDGE Every exposed surface of your refrigerator can play an active role in maximizing storage. On the top, organize drinkware, linens, and dishes in well-chosen containers such as silverware caddies and sturdy baskets. In the Cottage, we opted for wire bins; their see-through sides keep the room looking airy and help us see instantly where something is located. On the door and side panels of the fridge, we store an array of items, including measuring charts, serving utensils, aprons, pot holders, and dish towels. (Make sure anything on the door can withstand it opening and closing without falling off.)

DRY IN THE DISHWASHER If you have a dishwasher, it can come in handy even when it's not in a wash cycle. Households of one or two people may not need to run the dishwasher often, especially if you choose to clean utensils and plates by hand as you dirty them. If so, use the top compartment of the washer as a drying rack and skip the countertop model.

096 Free Up Counters with Magnets

The magnetized strip may be the best kitchen storage invention of all time. It's also spawned a whole host of products that help you keep tools and ingredients handy while removing them from your countertops.

GO WITH THE CLASSIC A magnetic knife strip affixed in the space between the counter and overhead cabinets holds knives and other metal cooking tools within arm's reach near your stove or sink. Stick it to your backsplash with heavy-duty damage-free adhesive strips.

RACK IT UP Magnetic organization racks can easily support small shelves for spices, coffee filters, coasters, medicines, measuring spoons, matches, bottle openers, and more. Just make sure they're securely fastened to your wall, backsplash, or even your fridge.

STORE IN YOUR SINK If the area around your sink is always spilling over with bottles, brushes,

and sponges, consider stashing those items in a magnetic caddy within your sink. (For a ceramic sink, use one with a suction cup.) If you need to access your entire basin, simply pop the caddy off the sink wall.

FIND MAGNETIZED TOOLS If your appliances are metal, forgo the rack or caddy in favor of magnetized tools. Timers, thermometers, measuring spoons, bottle openers, and even dish towels with a tiny magnet in the corner let you store them on any metal surface.

It's hard to experience the joy of cooking when you've got 1 foot (30 cm) or less of working counter space, or just a single drawer to store the useful tools that make cooking enjoyable. While creating storage solutions is key, it's equally important to purchase small-space-friendly implements to begin with.

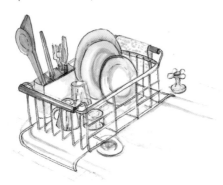

097 Dry Dishes Over the Sink

Why waste meal-prep surface area on a dish rack? Find one that straddles the sink but leaves ample space to pour a glass of water or rinse a dish. Bonus points for collapsible silicone models you can flatten and store.

098 Nest Everything— Even Spatulas

Nesting bowls are magical space-savers: Their descending sizes allow them to sit inside each other, Russian-doll-style. Look for this design feature in other kitchen goods, such as measuring spoons, food storage containers, and utensil sets.

099 Expand Meal-Prep Surface Area

When it's not cooking up something good, put the stovetop to use with an over-the-range cutting board. These modified wooden slabs have risers on two sides to provide clearance over the burners and allow for steady cutting.

100 Opt for Pots with Detachable Handles

Thank backpackers for these clever nesting vessels, which have handles that snap off for low-profile storage. You can likely make do with one or two pans and pots instead of a whole set. Store them in your oven when it's off.

101 Brew Coffee with a Pour-Over Mug Combo

While coffee is a crucial component of many people's morning routines, full-size 10-cup (2.3-L) electric coffeepots and even single-brew appliances eat up precious counter space. Opt instead for a handsome pour-over coffee mug set. You can stack and store the mug and filter in a cabinet when not in use. We love our handmade ceramic one.

102 Hunt for Mini Kitchen Appliances

Seek out compact versions of your favorite countertop appliances. You can find stand mixers and food processors that are 20 or even 50 percent smaller than the full-size models, or small juicers and blenders that serve up a single cup of juice, as opposed to a whole pitcher. Don't hold on to accessories that come with the appliance if you don't use them. If you do, stash separate components in drawers with items of similar shapes and sizes, rather than storing them all together.

103 Pick Multipurpose Cooking Tools

When you can, opt for small but ingenious tools that serve two or more purposes—say, a single measuring spoon with a sliding mechanism that lets you adjust to tablespoon, teaspoon, and so forth, or a bar multitool that lets you mix, muddle, and more.

104 Double Your Kitchen's Shelf Space

To increase the number of shelves available in your pantry and cabinets, go both high and low, installing a mix of shelving additions that either build up from the cabinet base or hang below. Mix and match to best suit your space and needs.

STACK A SECOND SHELF Don't leave dead storage space above your serving pieces or pantry items! Seek out shallow shelves on risers that let you create a second platform within a cabinet. Some units are stackable, giving you the potential for three levels.

SLIDE OUT SHELVES Mostly available in wood, ingenious pullout shelf units are affordable and easy to install in standard cabinets. They allow you to maximize vertical space and find objects at a glance instead of stooping and crawling deep inside your cabinets in search of a tool, vessel, or pantry item.

HOOK ON A BASKET These neat hanging baskets come with a hook that slides onto an existing shelf, granting you extra storage beneath the surface that's especially handy near a sink or an oven. You can find them in utilitarian wire mesh or more decorative finishes. Also keep an eye out for under-shelf racks for wine glasses, or seek out hook systems for dangling mugs.

105 Tack Storage onto Cabinet Ends

If your kitchen has an exposed vertical surface—whether it's the side of a cabinet or the ends of a rolling cart—you simply must put it to good use. Mount hanging wire baskets or a small rail with hooks to this otherwise ignored space; it's the perfect spot to store and display attractive cooking tools (like the vintage strainers and measuring cups you see here), pretty cloth napkins, lightweight cutting boards, a pot holder or two, and a brush for your countertops. You could even mount a low-profile wooden ledge on a counter wall and use it to prop one or two cookbooks, or an iPad loaded with all your favorite recipes.

106 Maximize Space Above Your Cabinets

Kitchens come with all different ceiling heights, but standard kitchen cabinetry is usually about 35 inches (90 cm) tall. This discrepancy often results in dead space above cabinets—which, if you're lucky enough to have it, you should use to your advantage. This ledge is fantastic for displaying attractive oversize serving vessels such as bowls or pitchers, or for storing your cookbook library. You can also line it with baskets to conceal linens, seasonal goods, and little-used items.

If you've parted ways with anything you don't use daily, dedicate this newly cleared space to objects that make you happy: a photo gallery, a row of plants, a collection of vintage toys, or treasures from a memorable day at the beach.

107 Go with Open or Closed Cabinets

The passionate debate among interior designers as to whether open or closed shelving is the best solution to all our kitchen storage needs is still going strong. On one hand, open storage is airy, streamlined, and elegant, and it allows you to display a collection of beautiful tools, ceramics, and glassware. Plus, you never lose anything, because it's all right there in front of your eyes. On the other hand, it's all right there in front of your eyes: mismatched mugs, less-than-aspirational plastic food-storage containers, packaged pantry items, chipped breakfast bowls, disposable party cups, everything. Open-shelving critics also point out that dust tends to accumulate more rapidly when your goods are all out in the open, and that grease and grime from cooking can build up if you don't have a range hood over your oven. As a compromise, some people keep cabinets open but go with glass doors.

At the Cottage, we opt for a mix: We store our prettier pieces on open shelves and our hardworking but less lovely objects behind closed cabinet doors. But in general, the discipline behind open storage is great to practice: If you must show the world everything in your kitchen, it will force you to pick beautiful dining and serving pieces, decant ugly packaging into more harmonious and refined storage containers, pay attention to form and color, and do a regular edit of your pantry goods to keep your shelves tidy and accessible.

Before installing open shelves, try removing the doors from your cabinets and test-driving the look to see if it works for you. After a few weeks, you'll know if you can keep the space organized and clean enough to warrant making the change.

108 Load Up the Backsplash

Take advantage of that strip of wall just behind the sink and under your cabinetry with some smart and eye-catching storage solutions.

HANG A WALL POCKET Utensil caddies for larger instruments can be overwhelming on the countertop of a small kitchen. By hanging a cone-shaped wall pocket or basket, you can keep your utensils within arm's reach without using up precious drawer and counter space.

USE SUCTION HOOKS If a tile or stone backsplash thwarts your plan for hanging storage systems, install suction hooks to the tile, or screw hooks or a rack to the underside of your cabinets and hang brushes, larger utensils, mugs, towels, herbs, and more. (Magnets can also do the trick; see #096.)

SET UP A RAIL SYSTEM We've all seen those efficient and beautiful kitchen-wall rail systems in magazines and online. The frustrating thing is that

these designs are frequently manufactured at far too big a size for tiny spaces. But there's good news: You can customize and adapt individual components to suit your space and maximize its capacity. Just buy or make a short rail to fit your space, then add S-hooks and hang mugs, towels, and storage baskets from the rail.

109 Solve Seating in a Tiny Kitchen

It's hard to carve room for chairs in a galley kitchen or one that's nothing more than a wall of appliances on countertops. At the Cottage, we have a breakfast counter that can fit two stools and a high chair between a pair of floor cabinets on either side, but there are plenty of other options if you don't have a countertop with room to spare underneath. Try a set of folding chairs in wood and leather that you can hang on the wall as decor when not in use. (See #138 for a version of this same idea coupled with a fold-out table.) Or, if you have a free wall with a window, mount a narrow shelf across it and slide two low-profile or even stackable bar stools underneath. You can also explore installing wall-mounted stool kits that either swing out or fold down. Available in industrial or modern finishes, these miracle-workers tuck back in when dinner's done—just make sure they're bolted to wall studs and can support your weight.

110 Pick Materials for a Tiny Kitchen

A kitchen remodel is not in everyone's forecast, I know. Whether you're a renter or a homeowner on a budget, you may not be able to remake even a tiny cooking and eating space. But some changes are relatively inexpensive to hire out or even do yourself. Here's what I've found makes the most impact in a mini kitchen makeover.

GO WITH BRIGHT SURFACES At the Cottage, we lived for six years with black-speckled marble countertops, which made the space feel cramped and dark to me. When we swapped them with a slightly textured white marble, the whole room opened up. While pale shades are always a good bet (see #013), don't rule out dark countertops. Just try them in a more reflective finish that will bounce light and make the space seem larger, like you see here. It also helps to pick thinner slabs for your countertops, as thick ones can make a space feel heavy.

BOOST DETAIL WITH TILE Who doesn't love tile? It's a great way to inject color and pattern into the backsplash area behind the sink. This goes double in a tiny kitchen, where you have to really pare down decor in order to maximize work surfaces. You can keep it fairly uniform with small tile in a repeating grid, or go with a dynamic pattern like herringbone. In the Cottage, we used 1-by-6-inch (2.5-by-15-cm) elongated rectangles, and their long lines help visually extend the countertop. If tiles won't work, try continuing the countertop material for the backsplash.

STREAMLINE FIXTURES Take a good look at your sink. Is your faucet design robbing you of surface area? In a small kitchen, go with a svelte single-hole model. So called because you only need to drill one hole in the countertop to install it, this faucet style incorporates the warm and cold controls onto one slender base. You can also explore wall-mount options and get the faucet off the counter completely! As for the sink itself, we opted for a subtle undermount style that doesn't interrupt the lines of the countertop.

111 Hide Storage in a Toekick Drawer

In a tiny kitchen, no nook or cranny should be overlooked as a potential storage solution. That includes the secret compartment behind the toekick—that funny recessed board under your base cabinets. You can install a drawer here that's perfect for baking trays, oversize platters, linens, and more. Order your new kitchen cabinetry with toekick drawers, or retrofit your existing cabinets with premade drawers (or built-from-scratch ones, if you're handy).

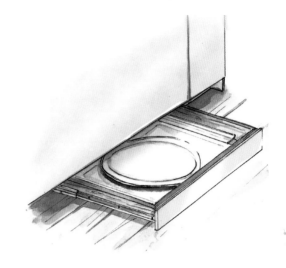

STEP ONE Pry the toekick loose and measure the dimensions of the cavity behind it. Standard base cabinets come in many widths—generally 18, 24, 33, 36, or 48 inches (45, 60, 84, 91, or 120 cm)—and are often 24 inches (60 cm) deep.

STEP TWO Your drawer will need clearance on all sides in order to slide in and out of the cavity. If you plan on using a drawer kit, search for one that's about 6 inches (15 cm) narrower and ¾ inch (2 cm) shorter than the cavity. If you're building from scratch, create a drawer box out of plywood and 1x4s. You'll also need a cradle for the drawer to slide in and out of; it should have ¼ inch (6 mm) clearance on all sides within the cavity. Once installed with the slides, the drawer should fit snugly inside the cradle.

STEP THREE If you're using a drawer kit, you'll likely need to secure a spacer to the cabinet's walls on both sides. To figure the spacer thickness, add the width of your slides to the drawer width, subtract this number from the cavity's width, and divide it by two. Cut two spacers out of scrap wood to this thickness and attach them to the cabinet walls with wood screws. The spacers should be at least as long as your rails.

STEP FOUR Use 2-inch (5-cm) wood screws to attach the drawer's slides to the spacers. Test to make sure the drawer glides easily on both sides. Install it inside the cavity.

STEP FIVE Use wood glue and nails to attach the original toekick board to the front of the drawer box. You may need to cut off the top of the board, working parallel with the grain, in order to make it short enough to fit under the cabinet again. Add a discreet handle so the secret is all yours.

112 Put Wall Cabinets on the Floor

Have an especially narrow kitchen? Get inches back in your floor plan with this ingenious hack: Skip base cabinets—typically 24 inches (60 cm) deep—and instead go with a bank of wall cabinets on the floor. These reduced-depth models don't jut out as much into the room, preserving valuable floor space while sidestepping the expense of custom carpentry. Most wall-mounted cabinetry models are available at depths of 10 inches (25 cm), 12 inches (30 cm), and 15 inches (38 cm); before you choose, check out the dimensions of your upper cupboards, since going any smaller than those could result in an unbalanced look. You'll also want to consider what you plan to store: If you have oversize plates, platters, or baking or roasting trays that you'd like out of sight, make sure your skinnier cabinetry can accommodate them.

113 Modify a Kitchen to Let Light In

Depending on when your home was built, your kitchen may not only be small, it may also be dark. In addition to using pale and reflective surfaces to bounce and amplify light, which will do a lot to open up your space (see #013 and #110), you may also want to consider a few contractor tasks that can help you let the sun stream into your space and make it feel larger (landlord and budget willing!).

The single skylight in our kitchen works wonders for bathing our cooking and dining space in natural illumination, and they can be relatively simple and inexpensive to install, depending on your architecture. I also adore our Dutch door (ours has a window in the top half), which we made by simply cutting our door in half with a contractor. The window always lets in some light, of course, but when the top is open onto the front porch, it brightens up our home immensely and also introduces new air flow into the room. You can buy Dutch doors at a home improvement store, or ask your contractor for a good local source.

SPOTLIGHT

Angie Wendricks

114 Meet Angie Wendricks of County Road Living

Angie and Alex Wendricks didn't just happen to find themselves living in a tiny farmhouse in rural Indiana—they saved and planned for six years to make it a reality. Known on social media as County Road Living, the Wendricks' abode is a spare-yet-homey, modern-yet-rustic open floor plan with lofted sleeping quarters, plus a garage. "In our county, you have to reach a square-footage minimum," Angie says. "Adding a garage was the only way to get from 700 square feet (65 sq m) to the 1,400-square-foot (130-sq-m) threshold. It was crazy."

Minimum square footage was just one of the quirks involved in building a home, the Wendricks found. Fueled by a desire to live more simply and cost-effectively, the duo wanted to do everything themselves in order to give it their own touch. "We chipped away at the cost of the plot and then paid cash for all the main construction, but we really did most of the interiors on our own—including the floors and building the loft bed and stairwell," Angie shares. "We were really winging it. YouTube helped."

Step inside and you'll see that the kitchen is prominently featured. Angie decided on a 15-foot (4.5-m) line of budget-friendly IKEA base cabinets, luxing them up with quartz countertops. She opted out of bulky wall cabinets, instead mounting a row of Shaker hooks for hanging utensils, pots and pans, and farmers' market baskets. Her ceramic serving pieces go on display in a beautiful shelving unit—an antiques store find with lots of texture and charm.

That's how most of the home was furnished: on road trips across Indiana, stopping in at estate sales and flea markets. Angie loves mixing rustic and even beat-up items—objects that seem like they have a story—with clean, modern lines in simple white. She also credits the home's uncluttered look to a few well-chosen pieces of larger furniture that provide storage (as opposed to buying lots of smaller pieces).

When pressed if she misses all the stuff we tend to accrue in larger houses, Angie is completely at peace: "I don't really get emotionally attached to things. You can still have your memory without keeping the stuff, and I feel more relaxed in a cozy, yet simple, space."

115 Embrace a Cozy Scandinavian Vibe

Angie is often asked if she secretly lives in Sweden, and it shows in her home's *hygge* (pronounced HOO-gah), a simple yet stylish coziness celebrated in Nordic countries—and pretty popular stateside, too. Her minimalist farmhouse doesn't feel uptight or severe; instead, it comes across as unfussy, honest, and inviting.

The best way to warm up a minimalist vibe is to include textured, tactile delights for comfort, and to fill your space with moments of dramatic beauty, like statement floral arrangements or fresh fruits. For visual interest, make sure the items you have on display are set forth in an eye-pleasing fashion, such as a deliberate pattern or a similarly artful format. For example, arrange homewares according to size or color, stacked and layered creatively, or evenly spaced in a grid. Symmetry is also a great way to make a space feel intentionally spare.

116 Tone It Down

I'm a big fan of white space—it calms the eye and allows statement pieces to shine. In Angie's home, this preference is taken to the most elegant of extremes, with her hardwood floors, clapboard walls, vaulted ceilings, kitchen cabinetry, sofa, dishes, and refrigerator all white as snow. It's about as zen as you can get! But she also breaks it up with texture and shine, like salvaged wood, both earthenware and glossy ceramics, nubby linens in soft grays and beiges, and metallic appliances.

When considering whether white-painted floors are right for you, be honest about your cleanliness (and that of your kids or pets, if you have them), and be aware that these floors tend to show signs of wear sooner than other styles. If you're still into the idea, do some research to figure out which materials and methods are best for your particular floor surface.

117 Craft a Kitchen Window Garden

Put your kitchen window to work without covering it up! Shelves over the window help expand storage potential and show off your personal style, all while maintaining that beautiful natural light.

Give some thought to what you want to display before deciding on the depth and spacing of the shelves. Small potted plants, ramekins, and glassware would be secure on shelves between 4 and 6 inches (10–15 cm) deep, and you can mount them anywhere from the windowsill to the top of the window frame. Deeper shelves for dinner plates and serving pieces should be mounted higher to keep you from bumping your head on them while working at the counter. You can also screw hooks to the undersides of shelves to hang mugs.

As for materials, wood shelves are easy to paint and mount on brackets, and they can support heavier items, such as dinnerware stacks or lots of potted herbs. Add stemware and other glasses to let light through and create sparkling reflections.

Glass shelves are also a lovely option. They make dishes, plants, and necessities appear to float—a delightful effect. While glass can safely support a good bit of weight, be sure to calculate the thickness of the shelf based on the length of window span and the weight of your objects.

118 Dangle and Dry Herbs as Decor

One way to get the beauty of botanicals in your small kitchen without taking up precious countertop space is to tie your favorite cooking herbs by their ends and then leave them hanging up as decor after they've dried. Dill, mint, basil, rosemary, and thyme all look lovely strung in a row like above, and their fragrance can linger and make your small space smell magical. All it takes is two hooks and some twine.

For a similar aesthetic, display a cook's wreath, a gorgeous collection of culinary herbs all woven together. Look for organic ones that you can use as you work at the stove, plucking bay or sage leaves and dropping them right into your pot.

119 Hang Essentials from a Window Frame

If you want to skip the shelf installation but still use your window for storage, try extending a metal or wooden rod across the span of your window frame and suspending a small potted herb garden, a collection of your favorite mugs, or an array of pretty kitchen tools. Or you can screw larger-diameter hooks into the top of your window molding, from which you can hang pans, pots, and smaller kitchen linens.

120 Display Fruit

You may think that living in a small space precludes you from cluttering up surfaces with food items—especially ones that can be stored in a nearby fridge or cabinet—and, in general, you'd be right! But I make exceptions for beautiful, bright fruits that enliven my kitchen and make it feel well appointed. A bowl of lemons, oranges, or apples can function much like a bouquet, and seeing them will encourage you to eat them instead of letting them go bad behind closed cabinet doors. A worthy use of counter space!

121 Set Up a Tiny Tea and Coffee Station

At the Cottage, we like to keep essentials for coffee and tea out on our breakfast counter so they're always at the ready. (Plus, no fumbling for your grinder and beans first thing in the morning before you've had caffeine!)

Set up a small tray or caddy that you can swiftly clear off a surface as needed, and make sure you tuck it out of the way of heavy traffic and activity. Kit it out with your grinder and French press—or your coffee-brewing instruments of choice—and a small bag of beans, or an array of your favorite teas. Have sugar and honey on hand, plus handcrafted stirring tools or filters. It also helps to have a cloth or two nearby to wipe up drips or spills.

122 Store Pantry Staples

When shopping for basic supplies such as flour, sugar, coffee, tea, cereal, rice, and pasta, try to buy as needed rather than in bulk for most items. This will ensure that you don't overload your storage capacity and will use up what you have before it has time to deteriorate.

If you're worried that you're spending too much money on single packages and prefer to buy in bulk, spend some time taking notes on your shopping and consuming habits so you have an accurate idea of what you or your family really

eats the most. For foods that you decide it makes sense to buy in bulk, I advise decanting at least a small portion into clear countertop jars or intriguing cruets so you have some handy for meal prep and don't need to dig out the bulk bin every time you need something. Your less attractive vessels can be tucked away in hard-to-reach spots, such as the top shelves of wall cabinets or in the very way back of base cabinets (or even weirder places, like under the bed or sofa). If you do move your dry goods or cooking oils far afield from the kitchen, it helps to keep an inventory so you don't forget what you've stored.

123 Weigh the Need for a Carbonator

Consider the pros and cons of keeping a water carbonator on hand. At the Cottage, we drink carbonated water daily, so we've opted to make room for a sparkling-water machine. It saves us money, keeps us from having to store prepackaged cases of bottles, and eliminates the need to stash bottles for recycling. (And think of all the waste it prevents!) When not in use, it either stays on our counter or fits in the taller cabinetry under our kitchen sink. But if you only use a few bottles a month, you can skip this appliance.

124 Take Your Eating Utensils on the Go

We try hard to avoid using disposable goods and single-use plastics when out of the Cottage. I carry a small washable pouch that easily contains almost everything we need for quick dining on the go. It includes reusable bags, bottles and thermoses, a bottle sling, camping cutlery for the adults, a folding spork for our son, cloth napkins, stainless steel and silicone straws (and a special cleaning brush), reusable beeswax wrap, and a waterproof sandwich bag in which to put the items after they've been used. It's all compact for toting and for storing in our tiny home.

125 Simplify and Refresh Your Eating Space

We all love the idea of a kitchen abundantly stocked with all of our favorite foods, as well as beautiful dining- and servingware, and the latest and greatest in kitchen tools. But in a tiny kitchen, you really have to make careful choices in order to prevent it from looking overcrowded. If you can avoid purchasing multiple sets of anything, donate your infrequently used kitchen gadgets, and only keep on hand what you use nearly daily, you just may find you have all the kitchen storage that you need.

COUNTERTOP APPLIANCES Blender, toaster oven, ice-cream maker, bread maker, panini press, slow cooker, stand mixer, food processor—the onslaught of single-job, stand-alone countertop appliances never ends. Yes, they're convenient and some have very small footprints (see #094 on miniaturized appliances), but in a small space, they can junk up surfaces and cut into storage space for food and daily-use items. If you don't use it once a month, you should let it go or find a truly out-of-the-way space to store it. This goes double for tools that perform a function one of your main appliances already offers—remember, you can use your existing oven for bagels, toast, personal pizzas, and more.

DISHES AND GLASSES The days of eight-piece dish sets and glassware for all occasions are long over. In all likelihood, you need only one set of four plates and bowls, four sets of flatware, and four glasses in two sizes (see #134 for more on the set we use in the Cottage). Each of these sets should stack so they take up as little room as possible in your cabinet. If it's chipped or broken, recycle it; if it's a novelty (like a mug you bought as a souvenir), limit yourself to one or two and donate the rest. If you find you have to do dishes more often to keep pieces in rotation, consider it a blessing in disguise.

CUTLERY AND COOKING TOOLS Unless you're a true professional, chances are that three wisely selected knives are all you require. A small paring knife, a general utility knife, and a chef's knife will cover most needs. As for steak knives, perhaps having two to four (rather than six to eight) could make a genuine difference in your storage space. The same principle applies to ladles, spatulas, and cooking and serving utensils. Choose versatile designs that will work with various types of dishes and occasions, reducing the overall number of tools you need. My list would include a slotted spoon, two wooden spoons, a slotted spatula, tongs, and a rasp grater. And don't even think of keeping duplicates.

POTS, PANS, AND MORE If you like to cook, you may think you need a ton of pots, pans, and roasting and baking trays in order to make your favorite meals. As a base for your cookware collection, you need only one large (10- or 12-inch/25- or 30-cm) skillet and one smaller pan—around 6 or 8 inches (15 or 20 cm), then saucepans in two sizes. Likewise, stock one deep and one shallow roasting or baking tray. (Bonus points for nesting models.) If you really love to cook something that requires a different vessel (say, a specialty cake pan or a stock pot for making your own soups), invest in just one or—better yet—borrow one from a friend or neighbor. Clean as you cook and this should be plenty.

FOOD AND DRY GOODS Every week when you go grocery shopping, clear out your fridge of last week's leftovers and not-so-fresh items before restocking. Once a month, survey your pantry and make a meal plan that allows you to use up any half-full bags or cartons, donating anything that's overstaying its welcome or tossing items that are past their expiration date. Once every year, take inventory of your spices and oils and get rid of any that have expired or seem unlikely to find their way into a dish anytime soon.

126 Roll Out a Secret Pantry

Most kitchens have a slice of unused space somewhere, and even a spare 6 inches (15 cm) by a fridge, an oven, or an existing cabinet can make a huge difference. Try this custom skinny rollout cabinet (at fridge or cabinet height) to maximize storage of canned goods, spices, or cooking utensils.

STEP ONE Measure for your pantry. For the length, subtract the height of a swivel-plate caster from the height of your fridge (or from the distance between the floor and the counter's underside, if you're installing a shorter model by a cabinet), then subtract 1½ inches (3.5 cm). Measure the width and depth of the space, too, subtracting ¾ inch (2 cm) from the width and 1½ inches (3.5 cm) from the depth. Use butt joints to assemble ¾-inch (2-cm) plywood into the open box frame.

STEP TWO To determine how many shelves you need and how much space to leave between them, first consider the height of the goods you'll store. Cut shelves out of plywood to fit, and use wood screws to attach them to the inside of the box frame.

STEP THREE On the inside of the box frame, drill holes for ⁷⁄₁₆-inch (1-cm) dowels, 1½ inch (3.5 cm) above each shelf and ¼ inch (6 mm) from the side edge. Secure the dowels in the holes with wood glue. Fasten two 2-inch (5-cm) swivel-plate casters to the bottom, centered between the frame's outside and inside edges.

STEP FOUR Cut a plywood backing to fit outside of the box frame. Decorate one side with contact paper, then use wood glue and finishing nails to attach it to the back of the frame and along each shelf. (You can also add a pegboard on the back of the frame and hang tools from hooks.)

STEP FIVE Cut a front face board from wood that matches your cabinetry. It should be the width of the box frame—plus ¾ inch (2 cm)—and the full height of the open space, so measure from the underside of the wall-mounted cabinet (or counter) to the floor. If your pantry is waist-height, consider a matching top face board, too: Make it as long as the top of the frame, and add ¾ inch (2 cm) to its width.

STEP SIX Align the front face board with the edge of the box frame side that will be closest to you when you pull it out, leaving a ¾ inch (2 cm) overlap on the back and top. Glue it in place and clamp until dry. Use finishing nails that are ½ inch (6 mm) shorter than the combined depths of the frame and face boards, working from the back so the nails don't show.

STEP SEVEN Apply plywood veneer strips to raw edges, and sand, seal, or paint. Attach a handle to the front facing board so you can pull it out with ease. Then stock it up!

127 Consider a Drawer Organizer

The world is full of drawer organizers that help you keep kitchen tools and cutlery neatly sorted. Here are a few styles.

GO WITH THE BASIC BOX Available in wood, metal, wire, plastic, and basically every material under the sun, the compartmentalized box is a mainstay. Try modular units that let you completely fill your drawers' precise dimensions.

OPT FOR A DIAGONAL If you have light DIY skills, you can outfit your drawer with diagonal wooden slats, which help in sorting kitchen tools by length.

ORGANIZE WITH PEGS To store plates or bowls in a large drawer, measure them and screw in pegs to hold them in place. You can update this system to suit your needs as they change.

GET CLEVER Not every drawer organizer needs to go in a drawer. Use the compartments to order and display any number of items—even try one on its side for a low-profile shelving unit, like you see here.

128 Pick a Waste Bin

Giving over precious square footage to something as unseemly as a garbage bin can be painful—with so few items on display in a tiny kitchen, your trash and recycling just don't make the cut as decor! If you can, conceal it completely under the sink in small cans, or donate a base cabinet to the cause and install larger pullout bins. If out on the floor it must go, seek slim dual-compartment or modular double-decker bins that store both refuse and recycling. You may find such an item to be a real eyesore, so consider hiding it in a tall woven or linen basket for a more subtle look. If you can't find something that's just right for your space, shop in unexpected categories. One of my favorite small-space hacks is repurposing indoor umbrella stands into a matching trash and recycling set.

129 Elevate Foil, Wrap, and Baggies

Boxes of foil, wrap, and zippered baggies can consume a phenomenal amount of room in your cabinets and drawers. Buy boxes individually as needed rather than in bulk, and simply tack the flaps of the cardboard packaging to the inside of your cabinetry, where they'll take up only open space. If the boxes are too heavy, use a nail or hook to hang a wire-mesh basket or a sturdy magazine file to the inside of the cabinet door. Deposit boxes of foil and plastic wrap in this clever new container while still using your cupboard as usual. (When possible, go green, using beeswax wrap rather than plastic. These easily folded sheets are reusable, recyclable, and compostable, so you won't feel as bad about giving them a permanent home in a cabinet.)

130 Corral Your Cleaning Supplies

Somehow, the places that hold our cleaning supplies commonly end up being among the messiest spaces in our homes. Try spanning a tension rod from wall to wall in the cabinet and hanging spray bottles of cleaning liquids over the rod by their nozzles or handles. Install a pullout tray, which will keep your bottles and cans upright and organized. (It may be helpful to store these supplies with a sponge or two in a caddy with a handle so you can carry it wherever disaster strikes.) Attach wire baskets to the higher sides of the cabinet walls and use those to stash rags, sponges, and other small gear. Add a few more tacks to hang brushes and a small dustpan.

It may go without saying, but positioning cleaners that you use for daily wipe-downs in the front of your storage space will prevent you from needing to rummage through more special-case items. Or consider arranging them all on a lazy Susan, which will let you easily swivel your collection of cleaning supplies until you find what you need. (See #230 for info on multipurpose cleaners.)

SPOTLIGHT

Christina Shirley

131 Meet Christina Shirley of Stella Blue Gallery

"Our home is an ongoing art project," says Christina Shirley, a jewelry maker whose penchant for layered textiles, eclectic yet earthy accents, and art collected from artisans all over the world makes her home a popular resource for fans of handmade and/or vintage home decor. Nestled on a small lakeside farm in North Carolina, Christina's 900-square-foot (85-sq-m) bungalow is also home to her husband, daughter, dog, and cat. The couple built the space when they learned they were having a child, intending to stay only a few years before moving to a bigger spot. Now, a decade later, they have no plans of leaving.

"For us, it just works," Christina says. "It's great with young kids because you're so close in the home—we didn't need an intercom, and we didn't have to follow our daughter around to make sure she wasn't getting into things. Even when her friends come over, I can hear what they're up to without constantly checking in." And Christina and her family do love to entertain: They've hosted up to sixty people at their small home, utilizing both the indoor and outdoor spaces for casual crab boils and birthday parties.

Christina's laid-back generosity translates to her decor, with a rich abundance of rugs, throws, pillows, and poufs keeping everyone comfortable, and a thoughtful collection of wood and ceramic pieces to spark conversation. And that conversation is exactly the goal: "If someone comments on a piece, I want to be able to tell them the story behind it. I want to be able to say, 'Our cutting boards were made by an Australian woman who selects and cuts her own trees, then handpaints them with a graphic design.'"

Nowhere is this aesthetic on better view than the kitchen. Open shelving offers ample display space for a revolving selection of art and curios, while the soy-stained concrete floors provide warmth and character. The family dines at a drafting table they found at an old lumberyard and cut to fit; Christina's husband sweetened the deal by making benches with wood salvaged from the same lumberyard.

Some may be surprised—or heartened—to hear that Christina's not an organization freak. "I'm the most disorganized organized person in the world," she laughs. "All of my messy pillows have to be perfectly arranged, and my askew rug must be perfectly askew. But if you were to look in my kitchen drawers, you'd see a bunch of stuff crammed in them." She advises going with the flow. "The more fun you have in your house, the better it feels, regardless of the size."

132 Layer It On

Many folks who live in tiny homes adhere to strict minimalism, but Christina's space shows that you don't have to go without. She packs in such a rich variety of artifacts: artisanal baskets and heaps of textiles, rugs, and pillows—many united by warm and earthy tones—as well as handcrafted ceramics, nutty wooden furnishings and tools, trailing plants, and a focal-point display of all her favorite vinyl.

So how do you make maximalism work in a small space? Sticking to a versatile yet cohesive palette is key. Notice that the main colors in Christina's home are brown and beige, punctuated with graphic black-and-white accessories. This is an easy commitment to make, and she's able to keep it interesting with an abundance of texture, muted patterns, and a little bit of shine (glimpsed in the appliances and the stained concrete floors). Not to mention, natural hues never go out of style.

133 Expose a Corner Cabinet

Why do wall cabinets get to have all the practical glory of exposed storage? The base cabinets can also get in on the action. Here, Christina's breakfast peninsula is cleverly left open on one end, displaying matching ceramics and coordinated baskets. This would also be a fantastic spot for cookbooks or any other items you wouldn't want on display above the range, where they can be affected by rising smoke and steam. It would also work great at the ends of a kitchen island, if you have one.

This space-savvy solution is friendly, too: To prevent ouch-inducing runs into the sharp corner, the countertop and shelves have been cut at a 45-degree angle. Talk to a contractor about whether your end base cabinet would be a good candidate for such a treatment.

134 Convert a Living Room into a Dining Space

With the growth of lifestyle brands and blogs, we're inundated with advice on throwing the perfect dinner party. Photographs of elaborate place settings and seasonally hued linens and flatware fill our screens, while catalogs featuring the latest trends overcrowd our mailboxes. It's almost comical to those of us in small apartments and homes. When it's tough to find storage for two placemats, how can you even conceive of layers of ever-changing tableware?

Great news—you can indeed dine comfortably in your tiny home, and even welcome others to join you. All it takes is a bit of finessing and an understanding that you don't need more stuff to create an environment that is tasteful and inviting. As luck would have it, you also don't need more space. Case in point: The main room of the Cottage is usually set up as a living room, but we can convert it into a dining room—with comfortable seating for six—in five minutes. Here's how!

SET UP THE TABLE When changing our space to a dining area, I first relocate our coffee table, which is a storage trunk containing our guest bedding. We added wheels to the chest, so now it rolls easily into our bedroom. In its place, I unfold one or two collapsible bistro tables, which are usually set up outside on the front porch we share with the neighboring cottage. The built-in couch operates as a banquette, and I turn my two desk chairs around and slide them up to the table on the opposite side. (An additional folding chair can be brought in if another place is needed.)

ADD PLACE SETTINGS I don't have different tablecloths for each season. Instead, I have neutral linen cloths that I use in myriad ways, depending on our needs. Sometimes we use them as throw blankets, but most often we rely on them as tablecloths. We usually eat off our everyday medium-size rectangular platters, regardless of whether we're dining as a party of two or six. This shape fits well on a small table and allows ample room for glasses, flatware, and decor.

TRIM THE TABLE Rather than purchasing new napkins and plates at the start of each season for an up-to-the-minute tablescape, I decorate the table with available flowers and greenery and then let the food take center stage. These simple choices immediately hit refresh on our tiny home, and I never have to store my holiday plates in the summer or stash my spring glassware in the fall. I save money, I save space, and I can flex my creativity and create a sense of occasion by using natural elements that are ultimately either consumed or composted at the end of the evening.

135 Honor Your Own Entertaining Style

This might sound silly, but I suspect that confidence—or lack thereof—is frequently at the root of so many design decisions when it comes time to decorate for guests. Find a style that makes you happy and works for your space, regardless of current fads. I love unbleached linen, low-key porcelain, unstained wood, and recycled glass. Products in these materials will work year-round. (I admire tables dressed in on-trend rose gold utensils and indigo napkins, but that doesn't mean I need to go out and buy those items for my little home.) Stick with what you find to be beautiful and practical, and add variety via your beverages, meals, and tabletop greenery.

136 Set a Tiny Yet Beautiful Table for Guests

Even tiny tables can be charming. You'll just need to make decor and serving decisions that beautify without cluttering up the surface so your guests can eat and converse freely.

ELEVATE FOOD The simplest of foods can result in a stunning table arrangement. To create a memorable setting that maximizes real estate, try raising one or more of the dishes on a cake platter or three-tiered tea stand. I've also introduced height with small upcycled wooden boxes. This clears room for plates, glasses, and decor while adding visual interest with multiple levels of food. (Of course, you can also move food off a tiny table onto a buffet to clear up space; see #137 below.)

SERVE ON SOMETHING UNEXPECTED There's no need to buy and store a lot of servingware if you can use a select few for several purposes. Skip the usual serving platters and oversize plates, and get creative with food-safe surfaces that you use regularly. For instance, instead of lots of small plates, group small servings on one pretty cutting board and the table won't appear so busy.

UPCYCLE JARS FOR DECOR Rather than storing additional decorative items (such as vases and candleholders), wash and repurpose your latest used glass jars and bottles to hold garden clippings and tea lights. (See #145 and #149 for more suggestions on candles.) Pasta sauce or pickle jars make wonderful vessels for centerpieces, while several smaller jars can hold a few sprigs or blossoms without taking up a ton of space. At the end of the night, just place the jars in the recycling bin.

PICK SMALL PLATES Full-size dinner plates can be anywhere from 9 to 13 inches (23–33 cm)—that's huge for a small surface. Try salad or dessert plates instead, which range from 4 to 6 inches (10–15 cm). Likewise, go with slim glassware—like a Collins glass—instead of fuller wine glasses.

137 Serve from a Buffet

Tiny homes can be wonderful gathering spaces. Such unique settings inspire a special sense of occasion from the start. But when entertaining in limited space, the practicality of serving buffet style increases tenfold. When guests can serve themselves, you're free to talk with them and enjoy the party, and this informal serving style also allows you to invite a few more people, since you aren't limited by table space. With a handful of helpful tools, you can quickly create a functional and stylish buffet, without upending your usual setup and without requiring extra furnishings.

USE WHAT YOU'VE GOT You don't need folding card tables to have a buffet—let your usual furniture assist you in your hosting duties. Desks, breakfast bars, kitchen islands, and coffee tables are, of course, excellent options, and all can be easily used to present food. Mantels, living room bookshelves, bar carts, media tables, and entryway consoles can also be just as effective.

CLEAR A SPACE You'll need to temporarily relocate some items when setting up a buffet on unusual surfaces, but this doesn't have to be an inconvenience. Simply stow your things in a box or basket, which can then sit cleanly on the bed—or even in the tub if you're really pressed for space.

DIY

138 Hang a Drop-Leaf Table on the Wall

For many, living in a small space means forgoing a kitchen table—not to mention the stately oversize dining room sets of the past. There are several wall-mounted flip-down tables available for purchase, but with easy-to-mount drop-leaf hardware, you can make your own table in time for dinner tonight—pretty much literally! Requiring a mere 30 to 36 inches (75–91 cm) of wall space, this simple slab surface folds down flat against the wall when you don't need it and then pops up to host a cozy meal for two when you do.

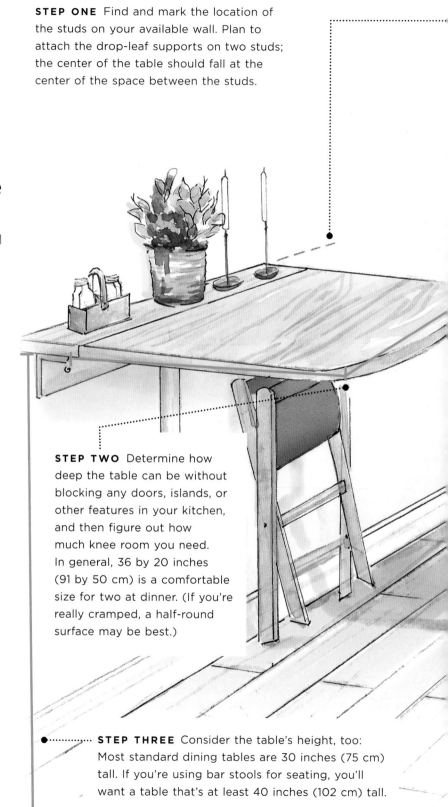

STEP ONE Find and mark the location of the studs on your available wall. Plan to attach the drop-leaf supports on two studs; the center of the table should fall at the center of the space between the studs.

STEP TWO Determine how deep the table can be without blocking any doors, islands, or other features in your kitchen, and then figure out how much knee room you need. In general, 36 by 20 inches (91 by 50 cm) is a comfortable size for two at dinner. (If you're really cramped, a half-round surface may be best.)

STEP THREE Consider the table's height, too: Most standard dining tables are 30 inches (75 cm) tall. If you're using bar stools for seating, you'll want a table that's at least 40 inches (102 cm) tall.

STEP FOUR Use a pencil to mark the ideal length of the table at the ideal height on the wall. Make sure to account for the thickness of your chosen tabletop—the top of the table's surface should be at your chosen height.

STEP FIVE Source your surface material. You'll want a tabletop that is finished on all edges, such as laminate-covered particleboard, butcher block, laminated oak, or walnut. Or you can buy a vintage or flea-market find and salvage its top, cutting it to fit your space if needed.

FOLDED POSITION

STEP SIX Select a set of drop-leaf hardware that looks nice with your table surface. (You can find many options available online, if not from a local hardware store.) Install these supports according to the manufacturer's instructions. To support the table weight without it pulling away from the wall, it's important to secure the hardware into the studs using wood screws.

139 Plant a Chandelier

Plants are the ultimate functional decor: While soothing us with their green hues and beautifying our rooms, they also breathe life into our spaces, filtering airborne toxins, reducing carbon dioxide, and even curtailing dust. If you want to add greenery to your home but can't find surfaces on which to place pots or stands, try suspending your plants instead. (See #140 for more on this idea.) Standard hanging baskets and macramé holders can be lovely, but there are many marvelous, free-spirited options, too—such as this chandelier repurposed into a hanging planter. It's perfect as a statement piece over your dining space.

STEP ONE Find a small faux-candle chandelier with saucerlike drip pans (called bobeches) that are large enough to hold one small pot each.

STEP TWO Remove the wiring from the fixture with wire clippers. You'll also need to trim off the light bulb sockets and casings, which may require more substantial cutting tools.

STEP THREE Add double-sided mounting tape to the bottoms of the cleared drip pans, then suspend the fixture securely from your ceiling or a beam. Make sure you hang the chandelier in an open space where you won't walk or knock into it while setting the table or dusting the ceilings or even just walking through the room.

STEP FOUR Press your pots into the tape on top of the drip pans. Remove the pots to water the plants, or place a mini ice cube in the plant's soil and let it melt. You can also select drought-tolerant greenery such as succulents or airplants that will thrive with a weekly spray from a water spritzer.

140 Suspend a Centerpiece

I often decorate the dining table with small bottles of greenery and flowers clipped from the garden. Translating the same idea into a floral chandelier is easy—and magical. Having a centerpiece floating above the table immediately sets a festive mood while keeping the table clear for dishes, cutlery, and glasses. Herb-drying racks work great as frames for these hanging centerpieces—plus, they often come with mounting hardware. Here's how to set one up.

STEP ONE Look for vintage or vintage-inspired herb-drying racks (rather than cheaper contemporary plastic ones). Securely suspend the drying rack of your choosing from the ceiling. A simple hook will do the trick, as this display is quite lightweight.

STEP TWO Wrap copper wire several times around the necks of five or so small glass bottles, leaving 8 to 15 inches (20–38 cm) loose on each one. Try varying the wire lengths so you can hang the bottles at different heights; it creates a more interesting composition.

STEP THREE To help prevent bacterial growth, first remove any leaves that will be submerged in water. (A hint of citrus-flavored soda or a drop of vodka can also assist in preserving freshness.) Fill each bottle with water and clippings before wrapping the copper wire around its neck and securing it to the rack. When I can find a small-leaf vine, I drape it over the rack and let it trail. For a celebratory note, top it off with battery-operated twinkle lights.

141 Serve from a Side Table

If you find yourself running out of dining space but have no room for a larger table, relocate some accent furnishings from elsewhere in your home or garden. Counter stools, plant stands, ottomans, hanging trays, and rolling carts are all excellent ways to add a crucial few extra inches for bottles, tablewares, silverware caddies, and food. If you don't have room for the table itself, a simple board cut to your desired length and propped on any makeshift risers of even heights can work wonders. Just make sure it's secure enough for you and your guests to enjoy safely.

142 Make Dinner Parties Happen Anywhere

With folding patio furniture—or even a few cinder blocks and boards—you can create a functional, lovely dining spot in the narrowest of spaces. One of my cardinal rules is that nearly every piece of furniture has to work in multiple areas. For instance, I found this lightweight bistro set that fits perfectly in our living room, on our porch, and even in the pathway of our little garden. (When not in use, I simply fold it down and stow it out of sight.) To dress up this utilitarian solution, cover it in pleasing-to-the-touch linens and snake a river of greenery down the center; it provides an organic touch without taking up as much room as a traditional centerpiece. Nestle candles and bottles in the greenery for an integrated feel. We relocate a folding bench from elsewhere in the garden to create extra seating, and cover it with a cozy and soft sheepskin throw.

While it doesn't take much light to brighten up a tiny room, it can be tough to find a place for floor lamps, tabletop fixtures, and pendants—not to mention dramatic chandeliers. Luckily, there are plenty of stylish, low-profile, and inexpensive alternatives to traditional lighting.

143 Take Your Illumination with You

Hanging lights are a guaranteed space-saver, and a single-bulb rope pendant with a 10-foot (3-m) cord is actually all you need for the whole home. Simply unplug and move it around your home wherever you need light.

144 Hide Can Lights

Recessed lighting is perfect for tiny spaces. While they're easier to install if you're building, it's also possible to retrofit with recessed fixtures, even if you don't have access to attic space. Look specifically for stick-on or recessed light housings—some LED downlights are available as shallow as 1 inch (2.5 cm).

145 Mount a Wall Sconce

Small wall-mounted lights make perfect accent illumination add-ons, especially flush ones that don't project out into your small space. To make sure you—and your guests!—don't bump into them, install your sconces well out of the way. (If you go with a candle version, it's best to make it battery-powered.)

146 Rediscover Battery-Powered String Lights

Twinkle lights are all grown up. Today they come in a variety of tones, shapes, and finishes—my favorites are nearly invisible wires that give off a bright, warm LED shine. String them around your dining space, or gather the cords into open-weave baskets and hang them everywhere.

147 Swivel a Swing-Arm Lamp

These ingenious hinged lighting solutions hug close to the wall when you don't need them and swing out to the center of the room when you do—ideal for a dining space. They come with a variety of fixtures and treatments; you can go with a classic pendant in bright copper, like you see here, or try a bare bulb for a particularly minimalist look.

148 Seek Out Low-Profile Statement Lighting

Not every home has expansive 12-foot (3.5-m) ceilings—especially not tiny ones. But that doesn't mean you can't attract eyes to the center of your table with a bold lighting fixture. Keep an eye out for creative but largely flat or flush looks that are designed especially for low ceilings.

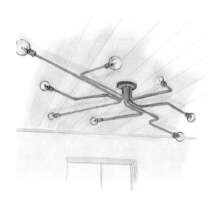

149 Opt for Sleek Candelabras

You may think that candlelight is out of the question on a small tablescape—one false move and you'll be extinguishing your meal, not enjoying it. Try looking for narrow candleholders and skinny tapers that take up less room among your plates and glassware, or place simple tea lights in a tray or glass jar for some (safe!) ambience. Or skip the purchase and just flip over an empty wine glass and put a votive on the upturned base for dramatic height—the clear glass won't crowd the table.

150 Host a Cocktail Party

Truth be told, cocktail parties in tiny homes are pretty wonderful. There's something about gathering in a small space that evokes a distinct sense of occasion. At the Cottage, we've hosted cocktail parties for groups ranging from six to sixty by using our indoor and outdoor rooms. As you make a plan for your particular space, keep the following tips in mind.

SET UP MORE THAN ONE BAR One central bar creates traffic jams—and in a small space, that backup can quickly take over the whole party. Try breaking up the bar into multiple beverage stations that guests can socialize around; for example, offer beer and wine in the kitchen and cocktails in the living room.

POST THE MENU To prevent guests from milling around in confusion, let them know their drink options from the start by placing a sign or collapsible sidewalk chalkboard at the front door, or near the coat and bag storage, so guests enter the party hands-free and ready for refreshments.

MIX SPECIALTY DRINKS AHEAD Upcycle a small basket, box, or suitcase into a special home bar by adding a few bottles of liquor, some basic mixing tools, a stack of glassware, and an ice bucket. Mix up recipes for two featured cocktails in smaller bottles, and voilà—you've created an instant happy hour in your tiny space. You can stash this improvised bar nearly anywhere, but do keep foot traffic in mind and leave space for guests to circulate.

CREATE DRINKWARE STORAGE Find clever, space-saving ways to stack unused and used glassware so it doesn't pile up around your tiny home. Fresh stacking glasses can be arranged on bar carts and counters, while a lower rack with clear signage is perfect for collecting used ones.

MAKE TOTING EASY Having your daily glassware, silverware, linens, and dishes organized into caddies will make setting up for events a breeze. Just relocate these space-saving containers from the kitchen to the table or bar.

151 Plan for Coats at a Party

One of the fastest ways to lose valuable surface space is for a guest to drop a tote or jacket on a chair, so be sure to have a dedicated and clearly marked space for your visitors' belongings. Near the Cottage's entry gate, I like to engineer a temporary closet by securing a piece of extralong driftwood or a pole to a pair of shepherd's hook garden stakes. Guests can then hang their bags from S-hooks and their coats on hangers. I also like to add a rug underneath so people feel comfortable dropping items there as well.

152 Put on a Momentous Event in Your Tiny Home

My husband and I were married at the Cottage. As such, hosting special events in small places is particularly close to my heart. We were engaged for two years before we finally set a date for our big day, because every time we attempted to start planning I found it too overwhelming. It wasn't until we decided to host our wedding at home that the process began to feel doable (and enjoyable).

I can now say from experience that hosting your wedding at home—even if your home is tiny—is an exceptional opportunity to make your special day that much more meaningful. Plus, it's a smart way to save money for your newly unified future.

You can apply the lessons we learned to any large event in a smaller space. Whether you're hosting an engagement party, graduation, holiday gathering, or birthday party, you too can pull off a happy and memorable celebration in a tiny space.

SKIP PRINTED INVITATIONS Digital isn't for everyone, but we loved it. About 80 percent of our guests replied almost immediately, and they could quickly click through to our wedding website for additional information. The digital approach involved no wasted materials, no time spent printing and addressing, no money spent on postage or stationery, and no stacks of invites piling up around the Cottage.

SKIP RENTAL CHAIRS Think twice before assuming you need to rent furniture. About ten minutes before the ceremony, we put out some of our regular folding patio chairs and benches for guests who needed to sit for our brief ceremony, and it worked perfectly. The majority of our guests stood through our vows. We said our "I do's" with guests on all sides, both in the house and outside in the garden.

HIRE HELP WHEN IT COUNTS Use your time and budget wisely. If you feel you need help from one experienced person, hire them for something dazzling. We hired professionals for one central decorative element: a fresh, natural botanical garland. This 26-foot- (8-m-) long arrangement lined the outside of our front door, where we held the ceremony. It performed as a traditional wedding archway, framing us as we shared our vows. It looked wild, alive, and absolutely gorgeous, and it made a huge impact while remaining appropriate to the setting. For the brunch and ceremony, we hired a bartender, along with a server who was also the busser and end-of-event cleaner. The two helped keep things tidy throughout the event.

153 Decorate Simply Yet Spectacularly

For our wedding, we wanted to keep our small space uncomplicated and natural. So we did what we normally do, filling our usual glassware with clippings and market finds. Adam and I opted to make our own arrangements (except for the garland above our door), and we spent about US$150 at the farmers' market in downtown L.A. That greenery was used for both gifting and decorating the Cottage—and we still had lots of leftovers! Sprucing up bland areas for events can cost hundreds or thousands of dollars, and it commonly requires delivery, staff, and coordination. Instead, we dressed up blank spaces (like barren exterior walls) with inexpensive beaker vases and unfussy yet dynamic branches from the flower market. It was simple and delightful to do together, saved us money, and fit our space perfectly.

SLEEPING

Bedrooms are sacred spaces. They set the tone for how we rest during our nights, and how we rise up to greet each day. Make yours a peaceful and practical retreat.

154 Put a Tiny Bedroom to Work

Bedrooms can be a tricky balancing act. On the one hand, they must offer comfort and a sense of calm; on the other, they must provide ample space for a diverse array of personal items. At the Cottage, we've achieved the best of both worlds with smart storage under and around our bed, and by making decorating decisions that help the space feel unified and relaxing.

The bedroom is my favorite area of our little home, and so much of that has to do with the bed itself. The ingenious space-saving sleeping platform and wall storage unit were installed long before we moved in, and not only do they make the room unique and peaceful, but they're also incredibly functional. The layout was inspired by a boat, which you can see in the bed (which has lots of storage underneath) and in the narrow window design above the headboard. These built-ins help us keep our lives organized while still providing a personal, welcoming feel every night.

STORE MEDIA WHEREVER IT WORKS Our book collection is made up of titles we love, works by friends, and volumes still on our to-read list. While we donate regularly and buy digital, we feel strongly about keeping these physical books, so we make sure they work as decor, too. To keep the palette harmonized in the small space, we remove the dust jackets from especially colorful volumes or cover the spines with bookbinding tape. We tuck in wicker baskets to hold other personal effects and let the occasional plant or two trail down between shelves for a look that's dynamic yet romantic.

CONCEAL WITH DRAWERS There are four drawers on either side of the bed. The top drawer

holds phone chargers, eye masks, and other valet items. The middle two drawers contain socks and undergarments, while the bottom drawer is dedicated to pet toy storage. Whatever works!

PULL OUT A TRUNDLE At the foot of the bed are two deep trundle drawers that provide invaluable storage space. One bin holds our son's toys, which would overwhelm our home if always left in the open, while the other serves as our hamper. This space would also be great for larger items, such as luggage or a vacuum cleaner.

TREAT YOUR SPACE LIKE A GALLERY One of the ways I make our bedroom feel especially homey is to continually update the walls with artwork that we love but that is low-key and subtle. We also use the vertical space to store everyday accessories such as bags, hats, and scarves. We've even mounted small baskets on the walls to act as catchalls for random personal items, keeping them off the nightstand. For lighting, I bring in a battery-operated basket pendant light from the living space and hang it over our bed in the evening.

MAKE IT COZY BUT MINIMAL I balance out all the utilitarianism of our bed with linens in neutral colors and patterns, plus the occasional throw for a dose of texture and visual interest.

155 Make Your Bed a Functional Haven

In a small home, the bed most likely provides the largest available surface space. As such, it's probably not just where you sleep—it's also where you pack your bags, change your child's diaper, catch up on work, read to your kids, fold your laundry, invite your guests to drop their bags, and so on.

MAKE YOUR BED To help perform the day's tasks with ease and provide yourself the space you'll need, make your bed every morning. Besides being scientifically proven to make you happier, this simple act will automatically make a central focal point in your home tidy and attractive.

STREAMLINE BEDDING Well-chosen linens can help your bed play multiple roles. Try using a bedspread that's monochromatic or lightly patterned, keeping the visual clutter to a minimum. Avoid a huge stack of pillows that you'll have to remove in order to use the bed's surface, and, in cool climates, use a single comforter instead of many blankets.

156 Pick the Right Bed for Your Small Space

The bed is one of the biggest items of furniture in any home, and in a small bedroom that means it might have to do double duty as a sleeping platform and a hiding place for clothing, luggage, extra bedding, and more. When you're looking for a bed, here are a few considerations that will help you maximize space and storage potential.

DOWNGRADE TO A FULL If you can bear it, going down from a king or queen to a full-size mattress will put a ton of square footage back into your floor plan.

PICK A TALL BED FRAME One way to make your ceilings seem sky high—and your bedroom larger overall—is to pick a bed frame with a high headboard. It will lead the eye up, creating the illusion of a loftier space.

OR SKIP THE BED FRAME COMPLETELY This is a matter of preference, but it's just plain fact that forgoing a frame will spare you inches at the head and foot of your bed. If you love the space-savings but would never dream of sleeping on a mattress on the floor, try a platform bed without head- and footboards. You can also fake a slimmer headboard by hanging a textile on the wall behind your pillows, or go with a more dramatic display of plants or framed art to stand in for a headboard.

BRING BACK THE TRUNDLE These were a mainstay in kids' rooms for about a decade, and then they all but disappeared! I say it's time for a comeback. The trundle bed has a pull-out drawer the same size as the mattress, and it's a perfect solution for either a second bed for visitors or extra storage.

UTILIZE STORAGE UNDER THE BED Some frames come with drawers built into the bed platform (like ours at the Cottage) or with a hideaway that you can access by lifting the mattress. Either is a great way to make full use of the bed's large footprint in a small bedroom.

STORE IN THE HEADBOARD Check out bed frames with cubbies or even a pull-out shelving unit hidden in the headboard. Bonus: These beds allow you to get items off the nightstand and stored out of view for a polished look.

157 Enhance Your Bed with Storage

Just because your bed didn't come with built-in storage doesn't mean you can't use it to keep linens, clothing, and more out of plain sight. Here are some helpful hacks.

PUT IT ON RISERS This trick has come a long way since its dorm-room days. You can now find elegantly designed risers and use them to create storage space under your bed. Wrap your frame with a simple, unfussy bedskirt to conceal baskets or bins, and you may even be able to skip a traditional dresser.

ADD PULL-OUT DRAWERS Seek rolling baskets or bins that complement your style, or add casters to stand-alone drawer units. Slide these under your bed for discreet storage.

USE THE FOOT OF THE BED If you have enough clearance, consider adding a narrow bench, shelving unit, or low credenza at the foot of your bed. (Some bed frames even have an optional shelving unit that you can add on.) Even two low folding stools or small ottomans would allow you a surface for dressing and laying out clothing.

158 Consider Lofting Your Sleeping Quarters

Sometimes up is the only way to go, especially in a micro apartment. Before building a loft bed, first make sure it works with your space—you'll need enough clearance overhead (at least 3 feet/90 cm) and a safe method of entering and exiting the bed. You may enjoy a ladder, but a narrow staircase, as seen here, is a touch more refined and easier to navigate. (Plus, these stairs are cabinets!) Also, remember to not put your loft bed close to a ceiling fan or other potential hazards. You can add a sense of privacy with a curtain or a low wall that doubles as storage. Sumptuous bedding to top it off will make every night feel like a real treat.

159 Improvise a Nightstand

The traditional bedroom setup—a big bed flanked by two nightstands topped with table lamps, phone chargers, and a stack of books or magazines—is unrealistic in most tiny bedrooms. But this can be a gift in disguise. Allow yourself to start from scratch, basing your design on modernity, functionality, and your habits and preferences. The result can be a unique and truly lovely room.

MAKE A SURFACE DO DOUBLE DUTY If you have a small desk, vanity, or dresser, place it beside the bed so it can double as a nightstand, eliminating the need for another piece of furniture. The tabletop can transition painlessly from day to night and back again with the help of organizing trays, caddies, or baskets. For instance, put your bedtime gear in a small box or open caddy that lives at the back of the desk or vanity by day but is reachable from the bed at night.

MOUNT A NARROW SHELF If your bed fits too snugly against the wall to allow for any kind of adjacent furniture, try a simple board or corner shelf as your bedside surface instead, cut to fit your space and mounted with any hardware that suits your style. You could also make your nightstand appear to float with blind shelf supports, or use hinged hardware that allows you to fold it up or down (see #138 for the kitchen table version). For an attractive vertical display with zero impact on your floor plan, try mounting small wooden boxes or crates to the wall. If you have even a few inches between bed and wall, it's easy to add hairpin legs to a custom-cut surface to make a skinny table.

EXTEND A NIGHTSTAND Sometimes we require more surface area than our nightstands can offer. Rather than buying more furniture, I made a hard cover that slides over one of the open drawers, doubling the available space. During the day, I just remove and store the cover. (You can have one cut to fit your nightstand drawer; make sure the tray is rigid enough to support nightstand items.)

160 Hang a Caddy on the Side of the Bed

No room for any furnishings beside your bed? Whether you have a metal, wooden, or upholstered bed frame, you can add a hanging bedside storage caddy to hold magazines, remote controls, reading glasses, tissues, and an electronic tablet. These soft, slim organizers have lots of pockets and either attach to the bed frame or have a flap that slides between the mattress and box spring to hold them in place.

161 Mount Shelves Behind Your Headboard

If there's no room at the side of your bed, consider the space behind or above it. You can increase surface area with a single narrow ledge that runs the width of your headboard, providing you with a spot for a water glass and book, or serving as a ledge for a rotating gallery of framed artwork or a beautiful array of plants. If the ledge is as low as your bed frame, make sure you won't hit your head or knock any objects off when you lean back against the headboard. (Check out #026 for advice on building a similar shelf behind a sofa.) If you can station your bed in front of a window, the sill can act as a shelf and you can skip the power tools!

If you don't live in an area prone to earthquakes, build shelves up to the ceiling for more storage and display options, but secure heavy items with quake putty, wherever you live. Paint the shelves to match your walls for a minimalist and tidy look.

162 Create Built-In Shelving Around Your Bed

Whether you call in a carpenter or pick up a hammer yourself, installing custom shelving around a platform bed is a great way to really max out a small bedroom or sleeping nook. Our bed was beautifully built decades ago, but the concept is timeless. Here's a way to achieve the look.

STEP ONE Measure your wall and the width of your mattress. Add about 5 inches (12 cm) to the mattress width to account for the bed platform. Next, subtract that total from the wall measurement to determine the span of your drawers and shelves.

STEP TWO Draw a rough layout, accounting for every inch from floor to ceiling. Let the height of your books guide how much space you leave between shelves, or calculate spacing to fit organizational inserts such as decorative baskets. Don't forget the thickness of your boards, and save 3 to 4 inches (7.5–10 cm) above the top shelf for crown molding.

STEP THREE Decide on shelf depth. For reference, ours are 12 inches (30 cm) deep. If possible, mount the shelves and vertical supports directly to the wall using pocket screws, eliminating the need for a thick wood backing. Make sure to mount your boards along studs in your wall.

STEP FOUR If you'd like drawers, first measure the internal width and depth of the nightstand. Then measure the width of one of your drawer slides, multiply it by two, and subtract the total from the cabinet's width. Have your plywood base and sides cut to this size for all drawers, then connect them with wood glue and nails along the joints. Sand it all down, then install the sliders in the cavity and along the drawer's sides. Finish the drawer with a face plate.

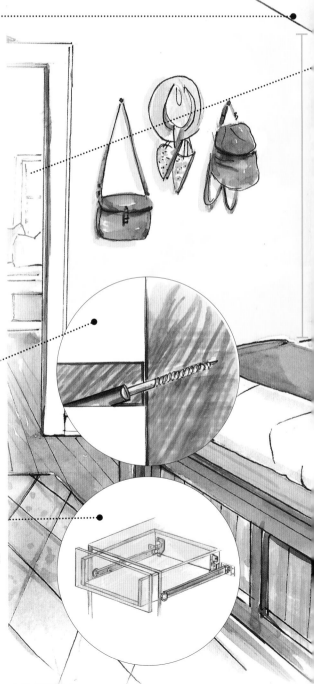

STEP FIVE Make sure to build the bed platform so your mattress is at a comfortable height. This is a task I'd encourage hiring out—especially if you want drawers in the platform. Our bed is a combination of plywood, 1x6 and 2x4 boards, and 2x2 posts, but you can opt for a simplified design. To create that true built-in look and provide the bed with a headboard, panel the wall and insides of the shelves with 1x6 boards.

STEP SIX Consider access. Here, 7-by-7-inch (18-by-18-cm) openings let us reach the light switch and water glasses on the bedside tables.

STEP SEVEN Finish it off. Keep in mind that a clear stain holds up better than paint. We did both, painting the shelf insides white but leaving stained wood on the exposed front edges and drawers.

163 Decorate Your Ceiling

If you're low on wall space in a small bedroom or studio apartment, look up to discover a large blank canvas just awaiting adornment. An elegant light fixture, eye-catching mural, or even just a pretty paint job in a slightly lighter hue than your walls will all draw the focus up, making the room feel larger, in addition to providing you with a chance to show off your style.

164 Go with Stylish Yet Calming Bedroom Decor

Your bedroom should be an oasis—a place where you retire for a good night's rest. As such, look for decor that is soothing and will make it easy for you to drift off to sleep.

CHOOSE QUIET COLORS When picking a palette, select similar tones to maintain a feeling of serenity and simplicity. Lighter, bleached colors will reflect sunlight, making your room feel more spacious. Save deep, moody tones for accent walls or simple, uncomplicated furnishings.

BE CONSERVATIVE WITH PATTERN Opt for comforters, quilts, sheets, rugs, and curtains in subtle, subdued palettes to avoid overwhelming the eye in a small space.

RAISE THE WINDOW TREATMENTS I advise skipping curtains or blinds—a sleep mask works wonders! But if they're a must, mount them at ceiling height to create the illusion of a loftier space, or use a tension rod to hang them up inside the window frame to avoid consuming wall space.

SOFTEN WITH TEXTILES One way to create a cozy nook for sleeping is to hang textiles on the wall or ceiling. Since they lie flat against the surface, they take up zero extra space and can inject a lovely dose of texture and color into an otherwise quiet room. Plus, they're easy to swap out whenever you want to mix things up.

GET LIGHTING UP Instead of the standard lamp on the bedside table, try sconces or swing-out wall-mounted lighting (see #145 and #147). A pair of matching lights on either side of the bed will also create eye-pleasing symmetry.

165 Multiply Your Bedroom with Several Mirrors

We've already discussed how mirrors can easily make a room feel bigger and brighter (see #013). They make even more sense in bedrooms, which tend to be smaller than main living spaces (and therefore even more in need of visual enlargement). And, since you likely get dressed in your bedroom, using mirrors as decor is practical, too. Try grouping several small, similarly designed models in a gallery wall to add dimension and style, or lean a larger mirror against the wall to create depth and lend an on-trend look. Add hooks to the sides or back of the mirror and it doubles as a clothing rack.

166 Insist on Creature Comforts

Bedrooms are more than where you sleep and get dressed—they're where you unwind, hopefully far away from the nag of digital devices and other people's needs. However you set up and decorate your tiny sleeping quarters, make sure it promotes relaxation. I have a wicker tray that I often use when I read in bed, perfect for holding a cup of tea or acting as a writing surface, which tucks away in a drawer when not in use. For breakfast in bed, I simply set up a tall plant stand alongside the bed and load it with drinks, food, and a petite jar of blooms. When accommodating more utilitarian items by your bed, try to find harmony between function and wellness. You might feel that you need to charge your phone next you, but perhaps skip the space-consuming charging caddy, and opt instead to tuck your devices into an accessible drawer. Swap a bulky box of tissues for an eco-friendly handkerchief. Corral your jewelry in an upturned seashell or a similar vessel. It is absolutely possible to make a small home feel as pampering as a weekend in a hotel. Life is short. Let's indulge in the simple joys.

167 Promote Sleep in a Studio Apartment

Sleeping next to where you eat gives some people real pause—waking up and seeing your sink definitely takes some getting used to! But humans are highly adaptable. Here are some tricks for surviving in a one-room home.

FAKE A SEPARATE BEDROOM FEEL It's nice to have a sense of privacy and retreat in the evenings. Try to set up your bed far from the front door or kitchen area, which will automatically make your sleeping quarters feel a bit more quiet and relaxing. You can also divide your space into entertaining and sleeping zones using furniture and rugs (see #021), remembering to keep the barriers low or transparent to avoid blocking light or sight lines. You can also

hang a simple curtain, or—if you're a light sleeper—mount curtain tracks around the bed and close it off in the evenings. You can also investigate turning your bed away from the room's more public functions and using your headboard as a dividing wall.

MANAGE NOISE If you live with someone, you know that when one person is up, the whole household tends to be up, too. While earplugs are your friend, it's important to establish boundaries for louder activities, such as phone calls and doing the dishes. When it comes to listening to music or watching TV, try implementing a headphone rule after a certain time in the evening.

BE MINDFUL OF SCENT It can be hard to fall asleep if you still smell dinner. Cleaning up, doing the dishes, and taking out the trash before bed will help, as will boiling lemon slices in water.

168 Appeal to the Senses

Our visual choices and decor can soothe our eyes and minds, but make sure to leave a bit of space to delight your other senses as well. Allot surface space for scented candles, small audio systems (see #068), and compact fans or heaters to assist you in achieving optimal comfort and relaxation in your bedroom.

And don't overlook the power of lighting—it has so much to do with your ability to get a good night's sleep. Look for slender fixtures that provide task lighting for reading, as well as accent options to create a cozy or romantic feeling. Go with a warm-temperature bulb—it helps you drift off to sleep.

169 Conceal an Eyesore Heating or AC Unit

A small room can feel even smaller if it has a permanent heat or air-conditioning source taking up a crucial corner—especially because these units tend to be, well, not the most attractive of appliances. Luckily, there are several DIY solutions that will help mask and minimize them. The key is providing enough clearance between the unit and your style solution so that air can flow safely.

BOX IT UP At the Cottage, we lived for five years with a 6-foot- (1.8-m-) tall exposed wall heating unit that stabbed at my eyeballs every day. When we made our closet into a nursery, we decided to deactivate the heater and close it off in a plywood box painted the same color as the rest of our room. Of course, this only works if you don't plan on using your heater—and you do involve an electrician to make sure it is safely decommissioned and covered. During the few cold days a year we get in L.A., we use a compact, energy-efficient space heater. I use the box surface to mount mirrors and other decor.

PUT A SHELF ON TOP You can have a surface cut to cover your radiator, effectively turning it into a small side table. Be aware that heat may warp wood, so marble or another stone is your best bet unless you can mount your board with several inches of space between it and the radiator. Hang

wooden slats from the shelf's edge, and you'll cover the unit while still allowing air to flow.

MAKE IT FURNITURE If you'd like to keep the unit functional but conceal it with an intentional look, build around it to create a faux piece of furniture. Lattice, slats, screen, or perforated board would look natural as the base of a sideboard or bench and still allow air to circulate.

PAINT IT For the simplest solution, give your unit style with paint. If you have an accent wall in a vivid color, choose the same hue for a camouflage effect, or try out stripes or ombre.

170 Keep the Bedroom Private with a Sliding Door

A door that swings into the bedroom will eat away precious floor space, creating an arc of unusable square footage. But a sliding model lets you keep a retreatlike feel in your sleeping quarters while maximizing your floor plan. Hardware kits for so-called sliding barn doors are readily available, and the look doesn't have to be rustic.

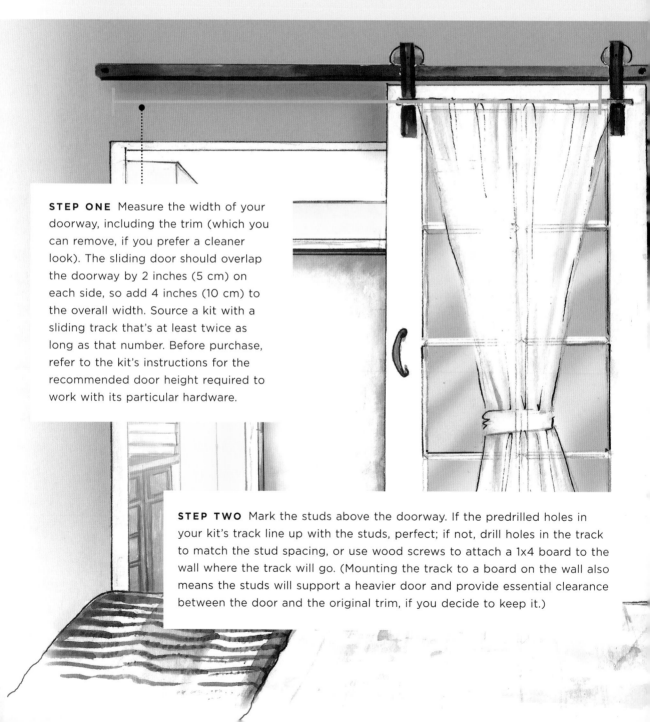

STEP ONE Measure the width of your doorway, including the trim (which you can remove, if you prefer a cleaner look). The sliding door should overlap the doorway by 2 inches (5 cm) on each side, so add 4 inches (10 cm) to the overall width. Source a kit with a sliding track that's at least twice as long as that number. Before purchase, refer to the kit's instructions for the recommended door height required to work with its particular hardware.

STEP TWO Mark the studs above the doorway. If the predrilled holes in your kit's track line up with the studs, perfect; if not, drill holes in the track to match the stud spacing, or use wood screws to attach a 1x4 board to the wall where the track will go. (Mounting the track to a board on the wall also means the studs will support a heavier door and provide essential clearance between the door and the original trim, if you decide to keep it.)

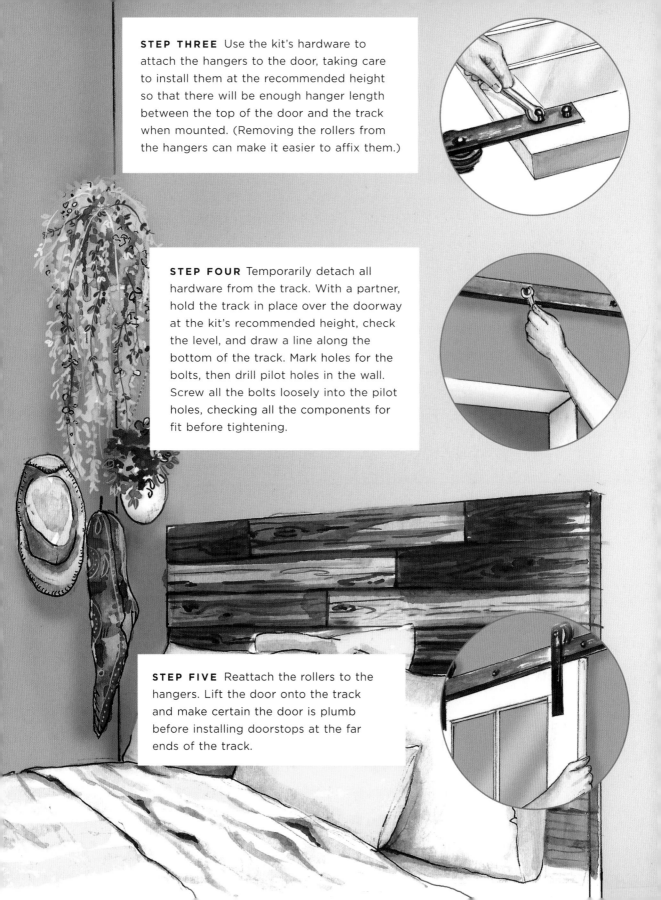

STEP THREE Use the kit's hardware to attach the hangers to the door, taking care to install them at the recommended height so that there will be enough hanger length between the top of the door and the track when mounted. (Removing the rollers from the hangers can make it easier to affix them.)

STEP FOUR Temporarily detach all hardware from the track. With a partner, hold the track in place over the doorway at the kit's recommended height, check the level, and draw a line along the bottom of the track. Mark holes for the bolts, then drill pilot holes in the wall. Screw all the bolts loosely into the pilot holes, checking all the components for fit before tightening.

STEP FIVE Reattach the rollers to the hangers. Lift the door onto the track and make certain the door is plumb before installing doorstops at the far ends of the track.

171 Meet Sheena and Jason of Mavis the Airstream

For Sheena and Jason, residing in a tiny space is just a way of living out their real dream: life on the road. After six years of marriage in North Georgia, the couple pined for their earlier adventures and travels in the American West. So they took a chance and bought a classic 1975 Airstream trailer—sight unseen. "We had never owned a camping trailer before, never knew anyone that had one, and really never even stepped foot inside one until we showed up and bought a trippy, shag-carpeted silver monster from a sweet old lady," Sheena recounts.

After two renovations and some 3,000 miles (4,800 km), Sheena and Jason—plus their poodle, Riley—had learned a thing or two about small space style on the go. "We lived in the trailer for three months and realized we'd made some design mistakes," Sheena shares. "We both worked from the Airstream, yet we only had one desk, and we had to crane our necks to the side in order to see the TV from the sofa. Also, we realized the original twin-bed configuration took up a lot of precious space."

Tackling all the construction themselves on not one but two occasions was a huge accomplishment for the duo and their family members, some of whom had caught the Airstream renovation bug. Since the sides of the trailer are charmingly curved, Sheena's father started joking that "building in an Airstream was like building inside of a fish bowl." The team replaced the twin beds with a full, switched the living and sleeping areas, and added two dedicated workspaces—one alongside the bed, and another by the media credenza in the main living space. Every inch was considered and built out, from the custom sofa, bed, and shelving unit to the bathroom doors. They also did all the electrical and plumbing work with no prior experience.

In addition to the impressive technical aspects, Mavis the Airstream is also adorable. It's outfitted with Midwest-inspired textiles, beautiful but small-space-minded plants, and wall-mounted art. The sleeping area—which overlaps with the tiny kitchen—is especially charming, with a fluffy cloud of a bed and a chic macramé arch overhead.

Sheena and Jason did sell Mavis in 2018, but they are now hard at work on a new Airstream project: Mavis 2.0.

172 Build, Don't Buy

One of the things I love about Mavis the Airstream is how Sheena and Jason updated nearly everything by hand. Even when they could have bought a piece of furniture and bolted it down to the floor, they more often than not elected to make it themselves. Case in point: Their TV console and storage unit is custom-built not just for the space but also for the items the couple planned on storing there—right down to their free weights! Painting the cabinet white to match the walls helps it recede in the space, creating a calmer presentation. Similarly, going with a white frame for the screen better camouflages the television, and a row of dramatic snake plants behind it amplifies the overall style while blending the tech, producing a feeling that is less stark and more styled.

173 Make Your Home Travel-Size

I always find that the perfect time to go through my closet and remove items I don't love or wear regularly is immediately after I return from traveling. There's something about having just made do with a small suitcase of clothes for a week that reminds me just how little I truly need. When they're out on the road, Sheena and Jason live this principle, keeping clothing and kitchen supplies to a bare minimum to maximize their space and focus on what's important: the experience of traveling together. The flourishes they do have are practical yet beautiful, such as a pendant light that lends texture and style through its macramé cord, and their personal effects, which often function as decor (see Sheena's hat hung right by the bed).

174 Fold Out a Bed

For some studio dwellers, it simply isn't possible to fit both a bed and even an apartment-size sofa in one room. (And let's be honest: Loft beds—see #158—aren't for everyone.) Day beds that can pass as a couch while the sun's out and provide comfortable rest at night are a solid option if you're sleeping solo. While there are loads of stylish designs on the market, it's trickier to accommodate a full-size mattress and frame. One fix is to revisit the pullout couch for daily use.

These space-saving solutions have come a long way since the uncomfortable monstrosity in your grandparents' spare bedroom. And the quality of today's air mattresses means that you can DIY a minimalist bed platform and top it off with an inflated sleep surface at night. This particular model—which we made for the cottage next door—consists of three identical platforms lined up side by side when in bed mode. And when it's couch time, you simply unscrew and stow the legs of two of the platforms, fold the bed back into a bench like an accordion, and top it off with custom cushions. If you embrace your limited space and collaborate with folks who have carpentry and upholstery skills, you can come up with all kinds of enriching fixes that won't even feel like compromises.

175 Configure a Dressing Area in a Tiny Bedroom

Ah, the closet . . . or lack thereof! This issue tends to be a common struggle among most small-space occupants—and it's often a big one for couples moving into a tiny home together. It's especially tough if you don't have space for a dresser or vanity, too. But if you're willing to regularly edit down your wardrobe and make good use of every inch, you can make it work.

I used to have a giant walk-in closet filled to the brim with rows of shoes, racks of accessories, piles of special-occasion garments, and hundreds of hanging items. When I think back about that now, I shudder. It was way more than one person ever needs. Fast-forward to my life at the Cottage, and I've learned to take in less and let go of more. While we relocated our clothing to an outdoor storage unit to accommodate our son's nursery (see #188), before his birth all our clothing and accessories fit in an alcove in our bedroom.

CREATE ZONES WITHIN Before West's birth and the subsequent conversion of our closet to a nursery, Adam and I shared a 3-foot- (90-cm-) wide stretch of dowel from which we hung the majority of our clothes on slim hangers. But your closet doesn't have to just contain hanging garments; you can fit your dresser inside, too. Beneath our hanging clothing we had sets of drawers and, to the left of everything, a narrow set of rolling drawers provided additional storage for folded garments, as well as scarves and hats. On the built-in shelf above it all, we tucked our winter coats and a few sweaters into matching bins.

SKIP THE VANITY You don't need a traditional small mirrored dresser with a matching stool at which to prepare yourself for the day. In a small space, simply move these activities to your bathroom, or use a mirror mounted to the wall.

CONCEAL WITH A CURTAIN For a peaceful, uncluttered look, we pulled a linen curtain over the closet when it wasn't in use. We also kept a few empty S-hooks secured to the grommets on the exterior of the curtain, and we used them to hold items as we're moving them in or out of the closet.

SHOP RESPONSIBLY Now, thanks to my small space, I'm mindful of every item of clothing I bring into our home. Was it made through ethical manufacturing? What are the environmental impacts of the process? How versatile is each item? Is the quality high enough for repeated use for years to come? Do I have another piece that serves the same function? What can I get rid of in its place? This might seem like a lot of effort, but it can quickly become second nature. We owe this consideration to the planet and future generations. And you owe it to your sanity to keep things streamlined and manageable.

176 Rethink the Closet

Clothing storage is one aspect of small-space living that my clients routinely bemoan. As always, my first piece of advice is to pare down your wardrobe regularly (see #175). I also believe you can craft a home for your essentials in any space.

BRING IN A WARDROBE If your bedroom lacks a closet, try a narrow freestanding wardrobe. Even a no-frills rack on rollers can get the job done, and you can move it as needed. (Wrap it in twine for an earthier feel.) You can even lean a ladder against a wall and use it to display tomorrow's outfit for a more rustic valet stand. When using an exposed wardrobe, be mindful to only display clothing in the same palette or aesthetic as your bedroom. Stash brighter items (parkas, socks, and so on) in lidded baskets. If you're using hangers, pick matching styles for a less cluttered look.

HOOK YOUR DAILY WEAR Clothing that hangs parallel to a wall takes up less floor space than it would in a standard closet setup. A Shaker-style row of hooks will provide easy access for daily-use items that, if mindfully chosen, can also contribute to the style of your home. No need to buy art to fill your walls—let your necessities do the decorating for you.

177 Give an Accessories Collection Pride of Place

Some people love handbags; others adore shoes. While I definitely advise scaling back to your most-used items, sometimes a collection of favorite accessories can make for a beautiful display in even a tiny bedroom. In addition to keeping these items handy so you use them more often and feel happy whenever you see them, displaying your accessories will keep them in better shape than shoving them in the back of your closet or the bottom of a drawer. Consider arranging all your shoes or handbags on pretty marble shelves, like you see here, or hang a striking vertical grid of hats on the wall.

178 Put Jewelry on Display

Much like showcasing your favorite clothing on the walls of your bedroom, a deliberately selected array of jewelry will illustrate your personal style. Hanging your jewelry on a series of small wall hooks or a sculptural rack is ultraconvenient and creates a striking visual. (Not to mention that the chains won't tangle.) Challenge yourself to declutter further by keeping only the pieces you have on display.

Clothing storage is key in a tiny bedroom, especially since there's such a wide array of items to store, from tall boots and roller bags to delicate camisoles and bulky sweaters. Mindful editing is essential (see #175), and a few of the smart tools here will help you organize—or even display—all your favorite garments and accessories.

179 Thread Accessories Through a Hanger

Scarves, belts, kerchiefs, shawls, ties—these little scraps can wad and twist up, wreaking real havoc on a drawer. Separate them out on a prettily crafted hanger display and you'll likely end up wearing them more.

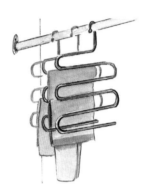

180 Store Pants or Skirts on an S-Hanger

Forget draping a single skirt or pair of pants on each hanger. Save space on the rack and maximize real estate below by loading up items on a tiered or S-shaped model. You'll also iron them less than if you folded them into a drawer.

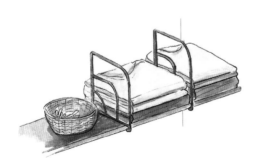

181 Create Drawers on Shelves

If you're low on drawer space, use shelf separators to create sections on high closet shelves, where you can stack folded T-shirts, sweaters, shorts, or jeans. Just make sure you can reach your most-loved items.

182 Hang Apparel on Decorative Hooks

When our storage items are delightful, we're more likely to use them—yes, even if they're in your closet. Hang items on an array of interesting hooks in hues and materials that appeal to you.

183 Double Up with a Tiered-Rod System

Put the space along the bottom of your closet to good use with a second rod for shirts and skirts. Most store-bought models dangle from the main rod, and some are even extendable to stretch the length of your specific closet. Seek out stylish versions made of wood or leather, or compose one yourself with a mid-level DIY project.

184 Suspend Your Shoes or Handbags

There are umpteen vertical shoe storage systems out there—from back-of-the-door hanging panels with pockets to simple hooks on a rail from which you can suspend footwear by the heel. Storing your shoes keeps them paired up and helps preserve them, so just make sure to choose the system that you're most likely to use. Bonus points for letting go of any that don't fit into your organizational model of choice.

185 Divide and Conquer Delicates in Drawers

Cut down on time—and frustration—caused by disordered dresser drawers with woven or linen drawer dividers. Available in various sizes, these cubes can be combined to fill out any drawer size, corralling socks, lingerie, T-shirts, scarves, and even jewelry into beautiful and ordered compartments.

186 Look High and Wide for Unused Closet Space

Even the smallest of closets can offer up tons of unexpected storage options. For instance, don't overlook the back of the closet door—it's perfect for a hanging shoe organizer or rails for scarves and shoes. Similarly, ask more of the walls: Simple hooks on the sides can be great for hanging belts, hats, and purses. You can also mount shorter hanging rods here for more clothing storage.

If there's room above the standard closet shelf, go ahead and mount another one even higher, or try extending high shelves around the entire closet (including above the door). Fill these shelves with seasonal items that you don't need for several months at a time.

187 Store Clothing with Simple Hacks

There are near endless ways to better upcyle common household items to organize your closet.

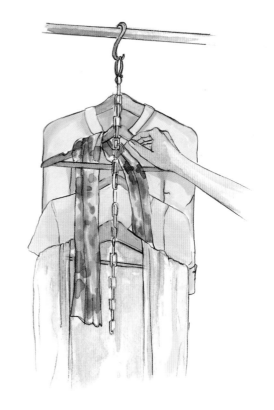

CALL ON CURTAIN RINGS Small wearables such as tank tops, bras, scarves, and ties can consume a shocking amount of closet space. But with the help of O-shaped shower-curtain rings, you can consolidate them all on the crossbar of a single hanger. Snap open a ring to retrieve or return items with straps, and pull scarves and ties halfway through, knotting slippery ones to keep them stationary. A flocked or velvet hanger helps keep the rings in place.

RECYCLE WINE CONTAINERS A six-pocket wine bag (often free with purchase) can offer the perfect low-cost solution for efficient shoe storage. Hang one on a side wall or the back door of your closet for easy access. If your closet is truly overflowing, consider purchasing matching canvas wine bags and hanging them on the bedroom wall. In a pinch, a sturdy compartmentalized cardboard wine box, turned over on its side, will also make a great shoe caddy on the floor of the closet.

MULTIPLY HANGING SPACE WITH A CHAIN The hanging rod of the closet gets crowded quickly when hangers are placed side by side, but you can save 6 inches (15 cm) of rod space by going vertical. Buy a 12- to 15-inch (30–38-cm) length of grade 30 chain and one S-hook at your local hardware store. Loop the S-hook over the closet's hanging rod and dangle the chain from the open hook. Then suspend multiple hangers on every other chain link, letting the hangers fall against each other and maximizing vertical space. You'll marvel at how much room you can save.

REPURPOSE BRACKETS You can mount standard shelf brackets on the inside wall of your closet and use them to increase hanging space. Try S-hooks with clips to hang pants, skirts, and more from the brackets.

188 Look Elsewhere for Clothing Storage

Thanks to the sunny, dry climate in Southern California, we were able to get creative with indoor-outdoor storage solutions, converting our bedroom closet into a nursery by downsizing and relocating most of our wardrobe to a 2-by-4-foot (60-by-120-cm) weatherproof cedar garden shed. It required getting rid of roughly half our clothing, but it was so worth it, and the process helped us get into the rhythm of making regular donations. We store infrequently used seasonal clothing—such as heavy winter coats and bathing suits—in two lidded plastic storage bins below a 2-foot (60-cm) rack of hanging clothes that we wear weekly, while our folded weekly wear was relocated to the storage in our captain's bed (see #162). Of course, your situation may be different—either in climate or available yard space—but the point is to be creative about where your clothing could go. There's no reason it needs to stay in a traditional closet! Try under your sofa—which is where our shoes now live, freeing up the floor in the bedroom closet for a small crib—or even in a garage. Just make sure your belongings are protected.

189 Simplify and Refresh Your Bedroom

There are countless ways to approach a wardrobe clean out, all of which are contingent upon your space, fashion aesthetic, and lifestyle. But—in keeping with the overarching message of the Cottage—let's keep this particular decluttering guide simple, shall we? Just sort your clothing, shoes, and accessories into the four categories below, and it'll improve both your space and your daily dressing routine.

☐ **DAILY WEAR** Your everyday pieces should also be your most accessible articles of clothing—try draping them from wall hooks, folding them in easy-to-reach drawers or bins, or rolling them to fit hanging storage cubbies in your closet. Keep only those that fit well, are in good shape, help you feel your best, wear comfortably, and are easy to stow. Believe it or not, you only need about three from each category (tops, bottoms, and dresses). Get rid of the rest. Excess eats up not only space but time spent searching through it. Any items at the bottom of a drawer or back of a closet likely aren't too special to you; place them in a giveaway pile and move on.

☐ **WEEKLY WEAR** Hang pieces you wear once a week in the closet or on a rack, or fold them into a drawer. Challenge yourself to keep this collection limited to a given amount of real estate—I make sure my weekly pieces don't exceed 18 inches (45 cm) when hung up in the closet. So if I buy something new, I have to get rid of something old. To cull your collection, make a few passes at it, setting things aside in a temporary "purgatory zone" for a day or two to test how you feel about letting them go. (I sometimes like to do this after a short trip, as I'm more likely to have a realistic understanding of what I truly need.) You can also ask a trusted friend whose taste you admire to help you part with old clothing with confidence. Having a second opinion really gave me the extra push to get rid of three times as much as I'd planned. And I've never missed a single piece.

☐ **INFREQUENTLY USED CLOTHING** This category depends on your geographical region and lifestyle. For me, this group of items includes bathing suits and cover-ups, slips, winter coats, heavier scarves, and formal wear. Since these are presumably pieces you use the least, or only seasonally, store them in the more inaccessible reaches of your home. For me, they go into a large bin on the floor of our garden closet (see #188) and in a garment bag behind all our other hangers. Try to limit yourself to two of each type. You're not using them often, and—since trends and tastes evolve—there's no need to store multiples.

☐ **GIVEAWAY PILE** If you have the time or would like the money, consider selling your clothing online or via local consignment stores. If an item has sentimental value, see if a family member or friend has a use for it. But the quickest and most rewarding option is to drop off these items once a month at a local donation hub, community-housing center, homeless shelter, or disaster-relief office. (Most of these places will also pick them up from your home for free.) Whatever you do, get rid of your discard pile as soon as possible. The longer you hold on to it, the more likely it is to grow. Even worse, you might be inclined to peek into the bags and pull out pieces here and there, allowing them to sneak back into your wardrobe, undoing all your hard work.

BONUS Try renting or borrowing clothing for special occasions and trips to different climates. This will cut back on what you need to store, while (temporarily) expanding your wardrobe.

190 Build a Freestanding Closet

Teeny closet or no closet at all? Construct your own open wardrobe with a narrow footprint and a polished industrial look using wood and plumbing pipe and fixtures. Try combining materials, such as copper with pine or dark charcoal-stained wood with galvanized pipe.

STEP ONE Plan your design around standard lengths of pipe, noting that you will need short lengths to go between shelves and two longer lengths to extend the full height and width. First, select wood for your shelves and measure the board thickness to determine how much threading you need at the ends of your pipe, keeping in mind that—when the pipe is inserted through a threaded flange and one of the shelf boards—the threaded portion should extend halfway through the board. Purchase unthreaded pipe and ask the retailer to add the required threads to the ends.

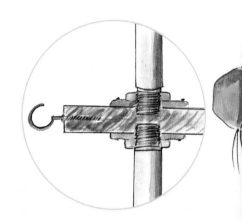

STEP TWO Make a template for where the pipe goes through the shelf and mark these spots on each shelf. Drill the holes so they're equal to the outside diameter of the pipe, which can differ from the pipe's labeled size. (Depending on your pipe's diameter, you may need a self-feed bit for your drill, or a hole saw.) Stain or paint and seal the shelves and let them dry.

STEP THREE Screw the threaded flanges onto each shelf, aligning one above and one below each pipe hole. Measure and mark spots for two casters on each side of the bottom shelf; use the mounting hardware to affix. Then, starting with the bottom shelf, position two of the shorter vertical pipes in the two flanges. Always dry-fit the pipe to the flange to make sure the heights are equal before applying glue to both the pipe end and the fitting.

STEP FOUR Position the second shelf on top of the first pipes. Repeat, ending with two shorter vertical pipes on top of the highest shelf. Dry-fit a 90-degree elbow to the top of the pipe on the left and a tee fitting to the pipe on the right.

STEP FIVE Mount and glue the full-height pipe on the right side; dry-fit a tee fitting to the top. To join the top, working from the left, insert the shelf-width pipe, the hanging bar, and the dressing bar extension—which provides a space to put your clothes out the night before—into the fittings. Once squared, secure with glue.

STEP SIX Use the bottom shelf for footwear and the shelves on the side for stacks of jeans and sweaters. Add hooks to the outer ends of the shelves for hats, scarves, and purses, and mount a full-length mirror on the wall near the dressing bar extension.

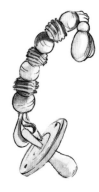

191 Set Up a Darling Mini Nursery

If you're expecting—congratulations! As you already know, everyone has an opinion on child-rearing, and your home will not be immune to this barrage of advice. Well-intended folks will tell you that you simply must relocate to a larger house—after all, babies require so much stuff. But living in a small space with an infant can be an immensely wonderful experience. People all over the globe raise children in varying types of environments, and if you want (or have) to make your small space work with a baby, you absolutely can.

My husband and I decided to get pregnant during our fifth year living at the Cottage. We knew that, with a bit of finessing, we could make our family fit comfortably in our small space; we never dreamed of moving to a bigger house. Here's how we made room for baby in under 400 square feet (37 sq m). (You'll see that we don't discuss a changing table here; see #196 for how to get by without one.)

CLEAR OUT A CLOSET Since we live in sunny and dry Southern California, we were able to relocate most of our wardrobe into a 2-by-4-foot (60-by-120-cm) weatherproof cedar shed outside (see #188). We repurposed the closet alcove as a nursery nook, removing the hanging rod but keeping the existing partition between the accessory and clothing areas. If you don't have a closet—or can't move your clothing outside—simply clear a wall or a corner.

FIND A CRIB THAT FITS The first piece of furniture we picked was a mini crib—and it was a hunt, as it needed to be a very specific size. Look for a collapsible model on wheels with an adjustable-height sleeping platform, which will

allow your child to safely climb out when he or she is old enough. (Some even easily convert into toddler beds, which is a nice cost savings.)

MANAGE BABY CLOTHES The only clothing, gear, and diapering goods we couldn't live without we fit in a tall wicker chest of drawers on casters and a few tiny hanging wire-mesh baskets. How did we do it? By only having supplies on hand for the age our child was at the present moment, not six months in the future or past. Edit your possessions routinely and don't stock up in advance, and you'll find that you need shockingly little storage.

GET STORAGE OVERHEAD We needed durable storage containers that were roomy enough to hold several items but small and soft enough to be easily pulled from the top ledge. (They also needed to remain secure during an earthquake.) Three gorgeous jute baskets did the trick, and a small step stool helps us grab them.

PICK ADORABLE DECOR I wanted the nursery to have dedicated decor that complemented the other art in our bedroom. A neutral painting and a dreamy handmade sail-away mobile won me over.

Newborns delightfully take over your life, but they don't necessarily need to take over your entire home, too. There's a wealth of wonderful dual-use and low-impact baby gear out there that will help you nurture your young one and maintain a clutter-free tiny space.

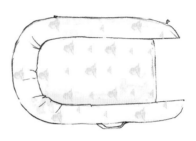

192 Inspire Play with a Collapsible Gym

Place your baby under a pretty pine mobile for hours of entertainment. Its dangling shapes help stimulate a developing mind. When playtime is over, simply fold it down and stash it for the next day.

193 Choose a Combo Bed and Changing Pad

Seek out a portable baby nest that allows for multiple uses, such as naps, cosleeping, diaper changes, and tummy time. Some designs come with a detachable toy arch that facilitates play. Multiple sizes and covers are available.

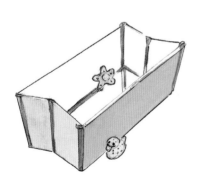

194 Fold Up a Bathtub

Sink too small for baby-bathing? No space for a freestanding baby tub? Go with a foldable or inflatable version that packs away when bathtime's over. As a toddler, our son played with his fold-up tub as a water table, too.

195 Use a Mini Nursing Pillow

Nursing pillows are extremely helpful, but their large size makes them a challenge to store in a tiny home. Try an arm pillow version instead; it helps keep you and your baby comfortable while nursing but takes up less space than more widely marketed designs.

196 Roll Up a Diaper-Changing Station

If you don't have room for a freestanding changing table, a travel changing pad can function just as well, and it can fold away in seconds. Look for one in a pretty fabric and print that has pockets for all your necessities.

197 Wear Your Baby

If you can help it, skip the massive stroller and wear your baby everywhere you go instead. Parents have been wrapping their infants to their chest for thousands of years. Besides saving space on bulky gear, it soothes your child to hear your heartbeat.

198 Hit Your Stride with a Supercompact Stroller

No storage space for a stroller? Pick a compact design intended for travel to use every day. Some models fold up to less than 1 square foot (930 sq cm) and weigh in at around 10 pounds (4.5 kg).

199 Grow Your Home with Your Child

We've found that the key to expanding our family within our tiny home is to evolve based on current needs. What worked when our son was a newborn was no longer suitable when he turned one. We enjoy this progression, and find ourselves excited by design possibilities that will accommodate his growth. There is no shortage of ways to make sleeping in a small space as a family doable: mini cribs, convertible toddler beds, approved bed-sharing docks or bedside sleepers, DIYs for outfitting a couch with a safety arm, Murphy beds, trundles, and endless custom designs—it's all out there. Work with your current stage, and welcome the changes that follow with open arms and creativity.

200 Deal with Limited Sleeping Spaces

Entire families have slept together in the same room for most of history—and many still do. You can absolutely make living in a small home work with kids—even teenagers.

CONVERT AN ALCOVE While we transformed our bedroom closet into a sleeping space for our son, you may discover other nooks that could make a good sleeping hideaway for a child in your own home. An under-stair landing may be the perfect spot for a crib or toddler bed (if the space is cordoned off appropriately), or consider lofting a walk-in closet to accommodate a sleeping platform above and a space for play below.

BUNK UP THE KIDS Little kids often share rooms, but there's no reason older kids and teenagers can't as well. In addition to space-saving double or even triple bunk beds, look into folding beds that will open up space for multiple uses during the day. Before putting two kids in one room, though, first consider their sleep schedules to ensure everyone will get enough rest.

CEDE THE BEDROOM For families living in one-bedroom apartments, it sometimes makes the most sense to let the kids have the bedroom—this way, they can sleep undisturbed in the evening while the parents stay up. Try a Murphy or fold-out bed that allows you to convert the main space back into a living area during the day. And make sure your mattress is comfortable; you need plenty of quality rest, too.

201 Sort Kid Stuff in the Bedroom

It's hard to keep a flood of toys from taking over your home, regardless of its size. But small spaces are especially affected by playthings' bright colors and materials. It's best to purchase beautifully designed, eco-friendly toys (see #074) and involve children in regularly donating outgrown items. Here are other ideas for keeping the flood at bay.

PICK ONLY ONE There's no need to buy toys, learning tools, or apparel in sets. Instead, let your children choose one item they love. For example, if your daughter needs a headband, don't grab a pack of five because that's what's available at the store. Instead, visit a website like Etsy with your child and encourage her to select one unique piece. This helps curb the number of items coming into your home, supports independent artisans, and encourages your child to take better care of his or her belongings, since they were hand selected.

STASH TOYS NEARBY Storage benches, drawers, and trundle-style rolling bins that pull out from under the bed are all hassle-free options that make it easy for your child to grab a toy . . . and to put it back! In a small home, your children have a unique incentive to keep everything in its place, because if they don't put used items back where they belong, they'll have no room for their next activity. If possible, let your child paint or draw on the interior of their toy storage unit, which will help it feel special. Pop-up hampers make great catchalls for temporary extra storage until you give away your excess.

BUY THE TRAVEL SIZE As your child grows, choose items designed with storage and portability in mind. Luckily, there are lots of games and toys available in travel-size versions that save space and are naturally easier to organize and stow. If it's good enough for the car or plane, it can work for a tiny bedroom, too!

SHOW IT OFF Once again, my go-to solution for storage is to line the wall. Musical instruments, athletic gear, and daily book bags can all be hung from hooks, making them easy to access and providing your children with a sense of pride in their hobbies.

202 Meet Jessica Helgerson

All homes have stories, but some have stories that are particularly long and rich. Take, for instance, this tiny residence: The 540-square-foot (50-sq-m) structure was built in the 1940s as rather plain sleeping quarters for workers in the shipping town of Vanport, Oregon. Then—after the town flooded—the small house was floated down the Columbia River to its present-day home on Sauvie Island, a bucolic bit of land just north of Portland, where it served as a goose-check station for hunters, of all things. When interior designer Jessica Helgerson and architect Yianni Doulis discovered its clean lines and ramshackle charm, they knew they wanted to make it a home for their family, which includes two children, Max and Penelope.

But first, there was some gutting to do. The two elected to thoroughly renovate the space, retaining its good bones and simple farmhouse appeal while making it more efficient for a modern family. They opted for one great room for the living area, kitchen, and dining room, which gets dramatic height and openness from the peaked roof. A bathroom and closet act as a divider, sectioning off the kids' room so they can sleep while the adults stay up in the great room.

But the real cool takeaway for small-space dwellers here is how Jessica and Yianni have built in sleeping surfaces wherever possible. The master bed is lofted above the bathroom, with a ladder that leads up and over a beautiful set of built-in bookshelves that span the house's entire width, which Yianni designed with a friend. "I was a little worried about feeling cramped," Jessica shared with *Martha Stewart Living* in 2012. "But I love the magic of crawling up to our own little pup-tent space." On the other side of the bathroom, the kids have their own sleeping space with built-in bunk beds and plenty of storage cleverly concealed behind clapboard walls. The bump-out at the foot of the beds is actually a pull-out closet, equipped with a hanging rod. Even the great room presents options for sleeping, as the built-in sofas function as twin beds for guests.

Jessica also wanted to make the space more eco-friendly, adopting reclaimed materials and energy-efficient lighting, and she wanted to give it a more playful sensibility, appropriate for their children. A "living" roof covered with moss and fern fit the bill. "It's mega-cozy!" Jessica reports. "And it's been interesting to see how little personal space we really need and how well we get along."

203 Carve Custom Nooks for Sleeping

We've already briefly discussed the joy of lofted sleeping quarters (see #158), and extolled the virtues of bunk beds for kids (see #200). But building them into the existing architecture is next level, providing a tidy, streamlined look. I especially love how surprisingly traditional Jessica's lofted sleeping nook feels. The cream sheepskin rug, pair of wall-mounted swing lights, and beautiful pitcher of flowers make the space feel less like a dorm-room solution and more like a farmhouse retreat in the trees.

204 Reclaim and Reuse Materials

I'm always a proponent of recycling, and I love how Jessica and Yianni redid their home with nearly exclusively reclaimed materials. Even the ladder leading to the loft is made of locally sourced walnut. While it certainly suits their self-sufficient lifestyle (they also keep chickens and bees on the property), you too can find ways to reuse instead of buying new in your everyday life. From repurposing wood for DIY shelves to visiting salvage yards for industrial storage solutions, these efforts give your home more character and are better for the world at large.

BATHING

Even a mini bathroom can be both functional and spalike. Streamline it for ease of use, then add a few touches of natural beauty to transform it into a soothing sanctuary.

205 Create a Fresh and Functional Bathroom Vanity

A tiny bathroom presents a host of challenges, especially when it's the only one in a household of two or more people. It's critical to hold the product deluge at bay in such a small space, but it's also important to allow a little zen to creep in: A few beautifying items on the wall or a shelf, your favorite scents, and lovely textiles should refresh and provide comfort.

The bathroom at the Cottage is by no means the smallest one I've ever had—it's not even the runner-up. But it's definitely compact, and it keeps us on a strict regimen of careful consumerism and regular weeding of little-used or expired items. There's no place to store miscellaneous impulse purchases here, and that's a good thing. Our bathroom holds a mix of health, beauty, and cleaning products for all five of us (pets included!), plus our guests. Rather than bumping into each other and getting annoyed, my husband and I cooperate with one another, instinctively polishing our family routine with every passing day.

LIMIT VANITY CONTENTS Our small sink vanity and medicine cabinet hold the majority of our bathroom products. The feature that gets the most use is the medicine cabinet. Since it is so small, every item inside must meet a list of requirements before landing on the shelf: Do we use it daily? Are its ingredients healthy? Is it responsibly and artfully packaged? Such prerequisites prevent goods from overflowing onto our countertops and set a standard for the remaining items throughout the bath. If it doesn't pass the checklist, we get rid of it, or—better yet—we don't acquire it at all.

KEEP DAILY ITEMS AT THE READY When approaching the organization and decor of the bathroom, I consider both efficiency and our temperaments. Everything we need for getting ready and out the door must be quickly available—wisely placed and untangled from neighboring items. My aim is to avoid scrambling to find, reach, uncover, or unpack something when we're bleary-eyed in the morning or when we're running late.

RESERVE THE COUNTERTOPS If an object makes it to the counter, it must be beautiful and useful. We keep this space pretty clear, but I often have a candle or other small-footprint decoration out for atmosphere, along with hand soap and lotion. You can press the windowsill into service, too—just be careful of getting the paint wet, which can create peeling.

CARVE LARGER STORAGE When you enter our bathroom, you first see an inset vertical shelving unit with six storage cubbies. At the bottom, I store our pups' dog food, then use the remaining shelves for a pail of towels, a first aid kit, my makeup supplies, and a small decorative sculpture. Everything is pale in color, blending in with the wall and creating a calm entryway.

206 Upcycle for Ingenious Bathroom Storage

You don't need to go out and buy the latest organizational tools created specially for a particular use—often, you can repurpose a vintage or more utilitarian general-purpose item to suit your needs. Take the humble hardware drawer, for example: One of the greatest things about these space-dividing tools is that they're available in dozens of sizes. Measure your space and find ones that work best for you. We have a tall, shallow option that fits in our base cabinet, just in front of the drain's U-bend. The transparent drawers are perfect for keeping my jewelry untangled and visible, which saves me time as I'm getting dressed and running out the door.

Need a bit more room for sink accessories? A vintage caddy on the wall frees up surface area while adding a touch of style to your bathroom. To liven up the look, try including a small draping plant in one of the caddy's corners. This unexpected twist can help beautify this handy little display.

207 Make Good Use of Bathroom Base Cabinets

In a tiny bathroom, the base cabinet can quickly devolve into a no-man's land of medicine, beauty and bath items, pet-care tools, and cleaning supplies. Invest time now in organizing and optimizing for daily use, and you'll save time later.

HANG YOUR HAIRDRYER Compared to most of the tiny tools in your bathroom, a hairdryer is pretty big. Its cord can also make it a bit of a pain to pull in and out of the cabinet every day. I keep mine handy and untangled by hanging it on a hook on the back of the base cabinet door.

BORROW FROM THE KITCHEN There are so many unique spice racks available—try repurposing one for your bath accessories! Store cotton balls, cotton swabs, travel-size products, and more within these practical jars and slot them into a rack below the sink. For storing other small items, install a magnetized strip (see #096) along one of the walls in your base cabinet and use it to hold hair clips, nail scissors, tweezers, and more.

GROUP STORAGE BY USE Sort your items by category into attractive yet resilient baskets or caddies, then stack them or arrange them front to back in order of most used. It's practical and will prevent you from mixing your hair products with your pet's grooming kit.

208 Streamline with a Mini Sink

We've become so conditioned to the bathroom vanity consisting of a large sink on top of a generous base cabinet for all our toiletries. But if you have the ability to affect your bathroom's design, one way to save space is to skip this traditional setup, opting instead for a narrow sink with a wall-mounted faucet. It will restore space in your floor plan, and I doubt you'll miss the larger basin at all. Skipping the base cabinet completely will also open up your space, making it seem larger. (Just be mindful of your plumbing; consider painting it for a more intentional and styled look.)

Conversely, if you're already in a home with a floating vanity and desperately miss the storage space, seek out or build your own custom base-cabinet solution. Keeping the shelving open will help preserve the spacious, airy look.

209 Be Strategic About Countertop Decor

Break the habit of buying miscellaneous decorative items and instead let pretty soaps, artisanal bath tools made of natural fibers, and other artfully crafted bath products that you actually use work as decoration. Consider decanting liquid soap refills into a lovely pump bottle, too. Once your basics are in place, add an upcycled glass vessel for greenery or a candle for a finishing touch. (You can also hang these items from the walls, shower curtain rod, or ceiling, as long as you keep safety in mind.)

GIVE BASKETS A NEW DIRECTION By this point, you've already learned that baskets are a small-space resident's best friend. In the bathroom, turn them on their sides and secure them to the wall for instant decorative shelving. This tip is particularly useful for larger items, such as towels and extra toilet paper, as well as flourishes like plants, candles, and artwork.

FLOAT SOME SHELVES There's no idea too basic in a small space. A clean, minimalist set of floating shelves—which have no visible hardware—will provide you with ample storage opportunities while taking up little visual space. Install them from floor to ceiling and stack towels, muted storage caddies, and jars of essentials. Select eco-friendly materials that speak to your style.

CRAFT A CUSTOM TOWEL ROD Skip the store-bought towel rack and make your own! Branches of driftwood are beautiful for this project; you can forage them yourself or buy them online. If driftwood doesn't fit your aesthetic, buy a wooden dowel from a local hardware store and have it cut to your custom length, then paint it to fit your style. With twine or wire, suspend the branch or rod from screw hooks in the ceiling. Add S-hooks for towels, jewelry, body brushes, or plants.

210 Style Toiletries in Creative Displays

Bathroom storage doesn't need to be purely utilitarian. Try more fanciful and textured displays that contribute to a sense of comfort and style.

211 Hang the Toilet Paper Roll Simply and Artfully

Sometimes small bathrooms don't come with a built-in toilet paper holder. Rather than buying another item, try a simple, charming, and unobtrusive DIY. Mount a simple hook on the wall near your toilet, then measure and cut a piece of twine long enough to make it through a toilet paper tube and still create a graphic triangle when hung on the hook. Thread the twine through the tube, knot it to create a loop, and slip the loop onto the wall hook.

Bathrooms are notoriously difficult spaces in small-footprint homes, as the lack of ample countertops and built-in storage tends to be a challenge. But there are countless smart products and storage ideas that help maximize space while keeping a retreatlike feel.

212 Suction It to the Wall

Get stuff off the countertop with organizational tools that stick right to mirror or tile, thanks to the power of suction cups. The toothbrush holders shown here mean you can skip the usual accessory next to the faucet.

213 Store Makeup in Hardware Drawers

Sand and repaint a small wooden hardware cabinet to repurpose it into a makeup organizer. It's perfect for categorizing your products (skin, eyes, lips, nails), and the dividers within each drawer are ideal for keeping items accessible. A vintage wooden sewing box would also work!

214 Stash Toiletries on a Skinny Cart

If you lack a vanity or are otherwise pressed for storage, look for a slim rolling cart—some are half the depth of their full-size counterparts, making them ideal for tucking alongside a sink or toilet.

215 Bring in a Teak Shower Caddy

My philosophy is to get rid of as many shower products as you can. But if you really do need a caddy, seek out one in an earthy material, like teak, instead of plastic. While you're at it, go with a body scrub towel in a natural material, too.

216 Embrace the Half-Round Hanging Basket

It's no surprise that I use tiered hanging baskets in practically every room of the house. But in especially small spaces like the bathroom, round baskets can take up a lot of wall space. For a sleeker solution, try models with semicircle baskets, which will sit flush against the wall. (Bonus points for ones in airy woven textures.) You can also separate them and use the single baskets wherever needed.

217 Create Storage Over the Commode

Don't let the space over your toilet go to waste. A set of baskets mounted to the wall provides helpful space for toilet paper, towels, and other toiletries, or you could seek out a specially designed multishelf storage unit that raises bathroom necessities up and over the toilet. (This lean ladder model is particularly practical.) Just make sure your storage solution provides enough clearance so you and your guests don't hit your heads on the bottom shelf.

218 Conceal Toilet Supplies

No one wants to see a plunger and toilet brush out on the bathroom floor, but sometimes there's just no other place to put them. Keep these eyesores close but out of sight in a quiet, low-profile caddy that fits beside the commode. Some even come in modern wood or marble, which not only look nicer but are often made using more environmentally conscious methods.

219 Simplify and Refresh Your Bathroom

The bathroom can conceal a shocking amount of stuff you don't use—from expired prescriptions to threadbare towels, from outdated makeup to duplicates of cleaning supplies that you didn't even know you had. But it's such a small space that getting it into shape should take no time at all.

☐ **PRODUCTS** Beware of bottle buildup! To cut down on clutter, evaluate which products you use daily. Are the ingredients safe for you and your family? Get rid of anything questionable. Next, choose just one bottle from every product category, then empty and recycle the remaining bottles. For unopened or lightly used products, ask your local community housing organization or homeless shelter if you can donate the items to their residents. (Some will even send a volunteer to your home for a pickup.) Simplifying creates a ripple effect: Fewer bottles means you won't need a shower caddy.

☐ **TOWELS** Everyday towels. Guest towels. Beach towels. Decorative towels. Gym towels. Fast-dry towels. The list of available linens goes on and on and is completely ridiculous for anyone in a tiny home. When clearing out the overflow, start with the washcloths. Do you use these, or do you instead use bath sponges and brushes? If you don't use your washcloths, get rid of them (and stop buying them just because they're available in sets). As for decorative or seasonal hand towels, if you're not actually drying your hands on them, they don't need to be taking up precious space. Donate them. Your regular everyday hand towels should be ones that you enjoy seeing and using daily. As for guest towels, your visitors will be fine using anything clean. Since you most likely have a few extras that you cycle through between daily use and the laundry, you probably already have enough for yourself, your family, and your visitors.

☐ **MAKEUP** Much like tackling your other products, take a fresh look at your makeup and cosmetics tools. Are the ingredients safe and not yet expired? Do you use the items regularly? Is the packaging pleasant? Throw out anything that doesn't get a yes. If you're clinging to a discontinued product, consider whether you really want to put those tired ingredients on your body. Are you holding on to makeup because you paid a lot for it, even though you don't use it? It's already a sunk cost. Let it go. Challenge yourself to replace five old items with just one product. Keep those selections organized in a manner that makes them easy to identify and access.

☐ **MEDICINE** Believe it or not, it's actually best to store medications in the kitchen instead of the bath, as the moisture from the shower can affect their efficacy. Regardless, keep them grouped and organized in a first aid box—lockable, if you have small children—which you can shuffle around the cabinets and countertops as spaces evolve. Make sure to weed out old prescriptions, as they can be ineffective or even dangerous to take past their expiration date. Consolidate first aid supplies like adhesive bandages on a regular basis, too, in order to do away with all the multiples that tend to accumulate when you buy supplies on the road.

☐ **COUNTERTOP SETS** Ah, bathroom vanity sets—more homes seem to have them than not. But before you go buy a matching toothbrush holder, liquid soap dispenser, soap dish, cotton ball jar, and paper towel tray, consider whether you actually need all of those things. Probably not. I skip these sets altogether. If you buy only what you'll use, you can save your premium counter space for daily use. For those who find they do indeed need containers, look around your home for items to repurpose rather than buying new.

DIY

220 Build a Vanity Between the Studs

Tuck an inset vanity between wall studs and cover it with a door featuring a full-length mirror, and you'll be packing in your favorite makeup and hair products without giving up any precious floor space.

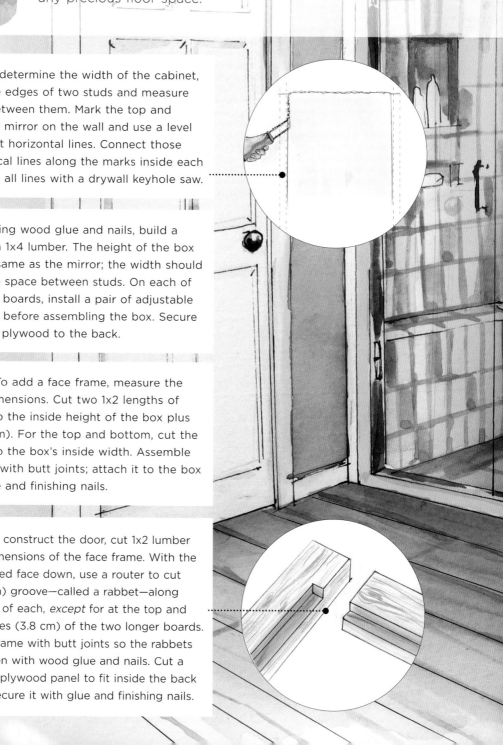

STEP ONE To determine the width of the cabinet, mark the inside edges of two studs and measure the distance between them. Mark the top and bottom of your mirror on the wall and use a level to draw straight horizontal lines. Connect those lines with vertical lines along the marks inside each stud. Cut along all lines with a drywall keyhole saw.

STEP TWO Using wood glue and nails, build a box frame from 1x4 lumber. The height of the box should be the same as the mirror; the width should be equal to the space between studs. On each of the longer side boards, install a pair of adjustable shelf standards before assembling the box. Secure 1-inch (2.5-cm) plywood to the back.

STEP THREE To add a face frame, measure the box's inside dimensions. Cut two 1x2 lengths of lumber equal to the inside height of the box plus 3 inches (7.5 cm). For the top and bottom, cut the lumber equal to the box's inside width. Assemble the face frame with butt joints; attach it to the box with wood glue and finishing nails.

STEP FOUR To construct the door, cut 1x2 lumber equal to the dimensions of the face frame. With the boards positioned face down, use a router to cut a ¼-inch (6-mm) groove—called a rabbet—along the inside edge of each, *except* for at the top and bottom 1½ inches (3.8 cm) of the two longer boards. Assemble the frame with butt joints so the rabbets align, then fasten with wood glue and nails. Cut a ¼-inch (6-mm) plywood panel to fit inside the back of the frame. Secure it with glue and finishing nails.

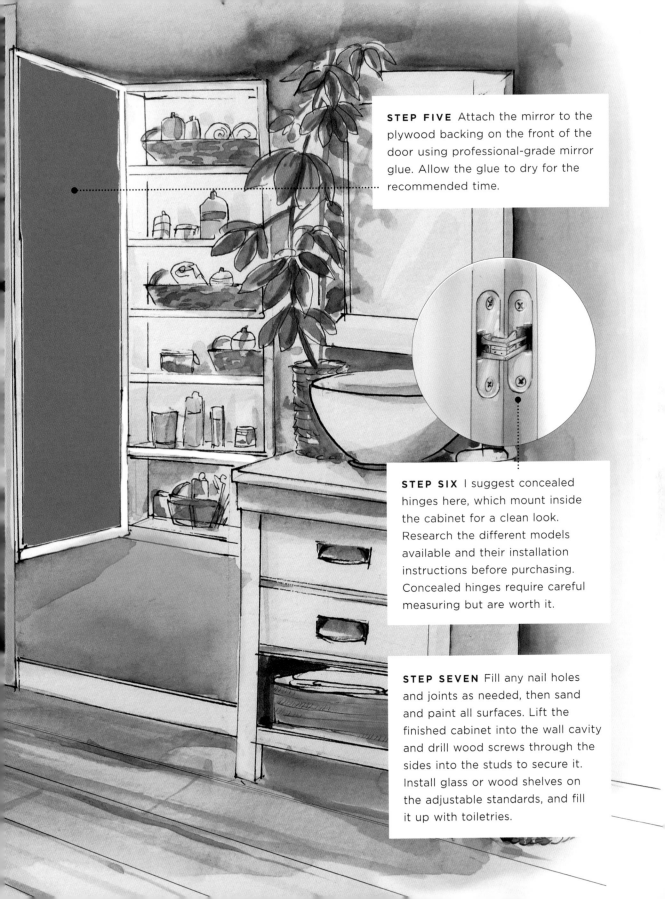

STEP FIVE Attach the mirror to the plywood backing on the front of the door using professional-grade mirror glue. Allow the glue to dry for the recommended time.

STEP SIX I suggest concealed hinges here, which mount inside the cabinet for a clean look. Research the different models available and their installation instructions before purchasing. Concealed hinges require careful measuring but are worth it.

STEP SEVEN Fill any nail holes and joints as needed, then sand and paint all surfaces. Lift the finished cabinet into the wall cavity and drill wood screws through the sides into the studs to secure it. Install glass or wood shelves on the adjustable standards, and fill it up with toiletries.

Spotlight

Susan Lennon

221 Meet Susan Lennon of the Craftsman Mini-Me

Our Cottage is my favorite tiny home in Venice Beach for personal reasons, but I would be lying if I said I didn't often dream about living in the nearby Craftsman Mini-Me. At 350 square feet (32.5 sq m), this charming spot is a real garden oasis, with vines winding their way across the interior walls and exposed pitched ceiling. In addition to generous windows throughout the space, the upper walls are completely lined with transom windows, inviting in even more light. Multiple French doors lead out to a lush yard and relaxing little veranda. Adam and I love to visit the Craftsman for staycations, as it offers the perfect pint-size retreat.

While the entire space is enchanting, the bathroom is an absolute showstopper. You first enter through the sleeping area, and after passing by a quirky mint green toilet, and stepping over an outdoor threshold, you find yourself in an overgrown and richly textured open-air bathing space. Enclosed all around with windows and walls that are thick with vines, it's outfitted with a rustic basin sink, a quaint mirror, an antique marble-topped side table, and a single hook for your robe. The bathing area is beyond simple: It's merely a showerhead descending from the vines 7 feet (2.1 m) above a tiled floor. There's really nothing more heavenly than an outdoor shower! And outside the lightly frosted glass windows, more vines and greenery provide lush privacy and endless appeal.

Created by designer-contractor duo Susan and Kevin Lennon, this craftsman dream feels intentionally left over from another time. "All the materials used to build our Mini-Me were recycled from salvage yards," Susan recounts. "It's very eclectic . . . We used a prison bunk bed for a couch and an elevator gate door as a room divider." While they do regular maintenance to preserve the balance of the bathroom, they've also experimented with letting nature reclaim it a bit, allowing the elements to weather the surfaces, and selecting pieces that will take the passage of time nicely. This approach makes it feel magical and unique instead of cookie-cutter, but it also takes the pressure off the furnishings and decor in a tiny room. When nature has decorated a room this beautifully, there's no need to donate limited space to accessories.

222 Lean Into Your Space's Quirks

This one-of-a-kind house just goes to show that a nontraditional setup can actually be a good thing—a great thing, really, when you work it to enhance your home's charm and appeal. While it's increasingly unusual these days to have an outdoor bathroom, Susan and Kevin didn't fight their situation. Instead, they made using a more makeshift arrangement a novel and desirable experience. (Of course, they're fortunate that they live in Southern California, where the weather is typically dry and warm.)

While the space is left spare to let the greenery shine, I do love some of the small-space-savvy touches they've incorporated. The vertical towel storage above the toilet is simple but effective, and the narrow antique metal stand tucked in by the commode is a far more lovely toilet paper holder than you could buy at a big-box store.

223 Consider Your Bathing Space

Whether you have a tub or a shower stall, you should relish the chance to make it your own personal heaven on earth. The key to having an enjoyable experience is a minimum of clutter—who really needs three different types of shampoo or two soap options? Pick only your favorites and forgo the rest, then beautify your space with a few lovingly selected flourishes.

Time spent in the bath or shower might be the only minutes during the day you get to disconnect from people and screens and truly relax. I view the shower at the Cottage as a quiet little getaway—a place where I am able to breathe and think without distractions—so I am careful not to crowd these precious moments with anything unnecessary. As such, I keep this small space set up for a simple routine that allows me to feel as though I'm in an almost meditative state of mind.

MINIMIZE THE BOTTLES Our shower contains just five items: a body brush, shampoo, conditioner, soap, and dog wash. That's it. That means there are only a few bottles to buy, replace, keep clean, and store. With so few items, there's no need for a shower caddy or waterproof shelving. Everything fits comfortably on our built-in tiled ledge, and I never feel as though the space is out of control. This simplicity keeps maintenance to a minimum when I'm cleaning and calms me when I'm bathing.

REIN IN NEW PURCHASES Knowing we have limited space means that the idea of trying the many sparkling new products that we pass at a point-of-purchase display in a store isn't appealing to us; we know there are better uses of our space—and our money. Our little house encourages us to keep this in mind, and it simplifies and improves our daily lives.

STORE TEXTILES WITH FLAIR Rather than just hanging our bath towels on standard wall hardware, we've suspended a piece of wood—salvaged from the forest surrounding my sister's wedding venue—and outfitted it with S-hooks from which to hang towels, plants, and decorative items, creating a display that is as sentimental as it is useful. I also arrange plants and other small items on our window ledge and from our shower curtain rod, never on a hardworking surface.

RECONSIDER THE BATH MAT The miniature size and often unconventional shapes of small bathrooms can turn sourcing bath mats and other traditional coverings into a challenge. Skip the usual bath mat, using instead teak or cork mats, which are often available in alternate sizes. Outdoor rugs from recycled materials are another helpful option.

224 Bring the Outdoors In

I love incorporating lush greenery everywhere I can—yes, that includes the shower! A curtain of trailing pothos plant over the window is a perfect way to gain a little privacy while not losing precious light—plus, it makes your home feel alive and verdant. You can also dangle a plant from your curtain rod, or place a plant on a high shelf. Just be sure to pick plants that like or at least don't mind steam and moisture.

Another great and low-profile way to instantly transform your bathing space is to hang a bunch of eucalyptus from the shower head. The hot water will bring out the eucalyptus's powerful and medicinal scent, making it a therapeutic experience every time you wash up.

225 Load Up the Shower Curtain

If you struggle with storage for your family's bath supplies, try layering a pocketed organizer panel over the shower curtain. Most models either hang from a strap attached to a slender wooden dowel or hook into the same holes as the curtain itself, and some come in nice materials like linen. You can also add a second shower curtain rod on the outside of your original rod and use it to hang towels and hand-washed garments to dry. Or, dry items from S-hooks threaded through the curtain's grommets or rings.

226 Create Storage in the Shower Stall

When it comes to storing your bath necessities, I encourage you to think beyond the metal or wire shower caddy hanging from the showerhead, which just says "dorm days" to everyone who sees it. Here are some more stylish ideas that may take up less room, too.

INSET CUBBIES In the Cottage shower, we're lucky to have an inset shelf below a built-in seat that stores our shampoo, conditioner, and soap. Such shelves are relatively easy to install if you're already retiling your shower, and they tend to be an attractive, minimalist solution.

ADD A HIGH SHELF If you don't have a built-in niche in your shower or tub, consider adding a slender shelf that can hold a few bottles. Tempered-glass shelves can stand up to the water and humidity but should be installed above the water spray. In a light or white bath, a vintage-style marble shelf with a rail would complement the tile. Glass and marble shelves all but disappear into the wall, creating a less cluttered look.

BUILD OUT A CORNER If you need a more robust shower storage system, consider building, not buying. For example, you can mount shelves every 6 inches (15 cm) along a narrow plank of salvaged wood. Secure the plank into a stud in the wall above the tile line and let it hang down along the shower wall, providing access to toiletries. (Just be sure to seal any wood you bring into the shower stall.) What other simple shower storage DIYs can you come up with?

227 Borrow Ideas from the Spa

If you feel the need to pamper yourself occasionally, you can do so with only a few extras. A fragrant votive candle or incense can transport you to another place, but indulge only if there's room in the medicine cabinet or nearby storage to stash it between uses. Bath salts tend to be bulky, but maybe you can fit in a small bottle of rose water, or add drops of essential oils—such as lavender or orange blossom—to your bath. If your herb garden is thriving, clip rosemary, mint, or sage and tie the clipping with a string, then toss it in the warm bath water, letting both the fragrance and medicinal effects help soothe a stressed mind and body without further encroaching on your limited bathroom storage. Another low-impact spa amenity you might enjoy is a small bath tray that allows you to read or sip wine in the tub; just slide it out of the way when bathtime is over.

228 Stock a Handy Cleaning Kit

One big benefit of a tiny bathroom? You have less to clean. Extend your minimalist mantra to include cleaning products by having only what you truly need to get the job done. As always, streamlining will save you money, space, and time.

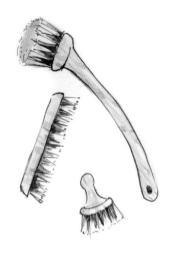

Prepare a small cleaning kit that you can stash under your sink, in a cabinet, or in freestanding storage. Include items like reusable cloths (old dish towels work great), rubber gloves, and one or two scrub brushes. I find it best to replace these items as needed rather than keeping multiples on hand, and I try to select well-designed, eco-friendly cleaning tools in natural fibers whenever possible. You may find you clean more often if you actually like your supplies.

Think about other ways to streamline your cleaning regimen: Can you skip the mop and wipe down your tiny bathroom floor by hand? Do you need to vacuum the bath mat if you can throw it into the washing machine?

229 Mix Natural Cleaners as You Need Them

Pantry staples such as distilled white vinegar, baking soda, salt, and lemon are useful for concocting effective—and all-natural—cleaning solutions. With these ingredients, you can make your own cleaning products in amounts that you'll use, meaning no more storing boxes and bottles of supplies. There are endless recipes online for natural cleaning solutions, so it's easy to find ones that work for your materials and preferences. Here's a primer.

MAKE A GENERAL CLEANER Mix 1 part vinegar to 2 parts water for a solution that can tackle glass, tile, and stainless steel. If you have mildew, spray undiluted white vinegar over the affected areas; repeat this regularly to prevent a recurrence. If vinegar's strong smell puts you off, add a few drops of essential oil to temper it.

MIX UP A SCRUB Baking soda is a mild abrasive that is good for both cleaning and deodorizing. Use it to scrub both porcelain and enamel tubs.

BANISH SOAP SCUM Mix 1 part salt to 3 parts white vinegar (or lemon juice) to scrub away soap scum in the shower or bathtub.

ELIMINATE RUST Make a paste with salt and lemon juice to remove rust stains around drains. This mixture also eliminates odors.

230 Choose One Multipurpose Cleaner

Why spend money and waste space on multiple bottles of specialized household cleaning products when you can select a single earth-friendly multipurpose cleaner? While you may want to stash a small bottle in your bathroom kit, you'll find yourself using it throughout the house. Liquid castile soap is a tried-and-true universal cleaner that is natural and nontoxic, so it's safe with little ones in the house. Squirt a small amount into a recycled bottle and fill it up with water, then use it for daily maintenance of bathroom (and kitchen) surfaces. Or keep a reusable glass spray bottle on hand and purchase a small container of all-purpose concentrate when needed.

Laundry is just a fact of life. In tiny spaces, however, wash day can quickly overtake the whole house, especially if you like to air-dry delicates. Here are some tips for keeping it all under control.

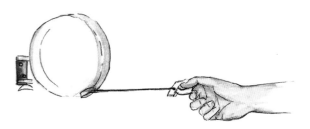

231 Pull Out a Retractable Clothesline

In a small space, a clothesline does not deserve pride of place! Look for a simple and small retractable line that you can unclip and store when not in use. (Or simply tack up a sturdy string!) It's ideal for drying clothing over the tub, but it's also great for small patios and balconies.

232 Decant Detergent into Lovely Canisters

Plastic detergent bottles are wasteful and can make a laundry station look cluttered and loud. Instead, pour your powders and liquids into nice bottles that you won't mind seeing. Consider collecting clothespins, sponges, and other laundry implements in matching containers.

233 Dry Clothes on a Collapsible Rack

A standard drying rack is hard to make room for in most bathrooms, but it's downright impossible in a tiny one. A wall-mounted collapsible rack lets you hang it up on laundry day and fold it away when everything's good and dry.

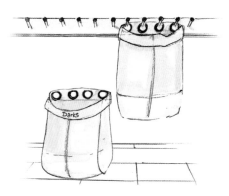

234 Hang Up Your Laundry Hampers

Hampers on the floor are more likely to get in the way and spill over, introducing last week's workout clothes into your living space. Try hanging yours from a hook on an interior closet wall or an otherwise out-of-sight spot.

235 Get Yourself an All-in-One Washer-Dryer

Why put up with two units when you can have just one? Washer-dryer machines make use of the same basin, saving you a ton of space. Most have functions comparable to those of their full-size, single-use cousins, and some can even hook up to a sink. This approach also saves you time, as the wash and dry cycles run back-to-back. Another floor plan–friendly option is a stacking washer and dryer set.

236 Fold Out an Ironing Board

Skip the floor or tabletop ironing boards and go with one that fits over the back of a door and folds down when it's time to press. Many models have hooks that allow you to hang them up and out of the way in a closet when you're done. (I've even used a board placed across the tub as a makeshift ironing surface— no stuff required!) You can also skip the old-school iron and opt for a travel iron-steamer combo—ours fits entirely in the palm of my hand.

237 Make a Simple DIY Sewing Kit

Spools of thread, needles, scissors, and more can wreak havoc on a junk drawer. Plus, they get lost easily, meaning they're never there when you need them. Solve both problems with the easiest sewing kit imaginable: a jar with a pincushion lid. You can make the lid out of pillow batting and a spare fabric scrap.

238 Conceal the Kitty Litter Box

No matter how much you love your cat, you probably don't love his litter box—it takes up floor space and is an unsightly reminder of a pretty unpleasant chore. But by downsizing your toiletries, you can free up the under-sink cabinet in your bathroom and hide the litter box inside. Cut a small door for the cat to come and go, and partition the space for storage.

STEP ONE Before clearing the cabinet under your sink, make sure it can accommodate a litter box large enough for your cat to use comfortably, bearing in mind that most cats need a box that's one and a half times their length. It's also important that there will be enough clearance between your cat and the sink plumbing.

STEP TWO Measure the fullest part of your cat's chest and its height from the top of its shoulders to the bottom of its chest. Add 1 to 2 inches (2.5–5 cm) to both measurements. Use these measurements to plan a comfortable cat door for an exposed end wall in your cabinet; consider a whimsical house shape to make clear it's intentional.

STEP THREE Mark the cabinet wall with the dimensions of your cat door. Cut the opening with a reciprocating saw or jigsaw, then seal the edges with paint or plywood veneer strips. (If you're a renter and concerned about permanent damage to the cabinet, you can cut into the door instead, which will be easier to replace when you move out. Don't want to cut into anything? Simply remove the door and hang a curtain.)

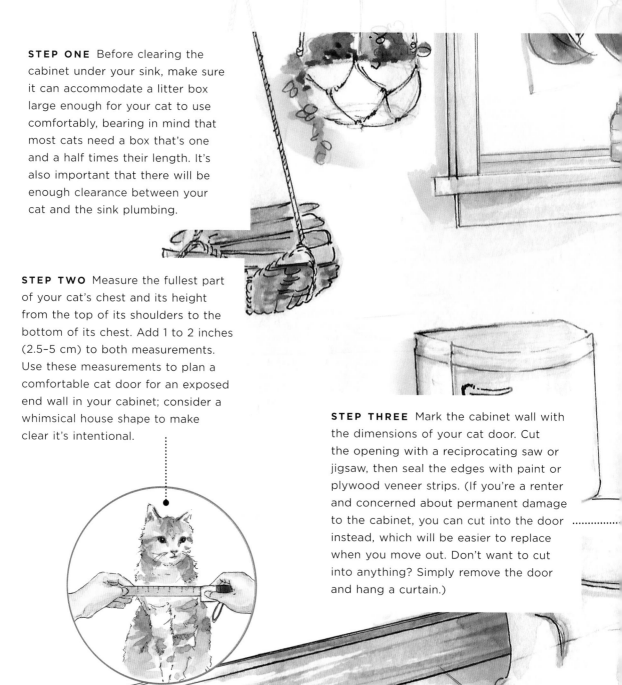

STEP FOUR If space allows, you can add a partition and shelf to separate the litter box from the extra cat litter, grooming supplies, and any other pet items. Cut a plywood board that will fit tightly within the interior walls, then secure it with a pair of corner brackets on all four edges.

STEP FIVE For the cabinet floor beneath the litter box, purchase a soft, easy-to-clean mat that will capture litter from the cat's feet. Screw small utility hooks into the walls for hanging a scoop, a brush, and a little wire basket to hold a box of baking soda, which will help eliminate odors. While cats can see pretty well in the dark, a small battery-powered night-light might help out your kitty.

INDEX

AUTHOR ACKNOWLEDGMENT

There's a lot of heartfelt appreciation swirling around this Cottage, and I would love to share my sincerest thanks to the many people who helped tremendously in the creation of this lil' book.

To everyone who contributed their imagery, stories, and/or time to make this title a diverse and worthy resource: Thank you for believing in it.

To my editor, Lucie Parker: Through every hour on the phone, every email, every idea, every hurdle, and every victory I've felt so lucky just to know you, let alone work with you. Thank you for going beyond.

To Katherine Pearson: You have unparalleled patience, grace, and positivity. I've learned as much from your spirit as I have from your delightful contributions to this work. Thank you.

Magda: Your ability to blend the technical and ethereal is nothing short of a miracle. These pages are beautiful because of you. Thank you.

To Molly Stewart, Jennifer Durrant, Lorraine Rath, and Kelly Booth: Thank each one of you for your time, creativity, and energy. You wove a path through tens of thousands of images and words from our miniature space to determine how to best provide a clear and concise direction for others.

To Lindsay Hollinger, one of my favorite humans and artists: Thank you for generously contributing that gorgeous handwriting of yours (which I've coveted since the ninth grade) to this book.

To Jaclyn R. Johnson, without whom I would be flat-out stuck: I am grateful for your guidance and friendship every day.

To Sideways Man: Thank you for putting up with your neighbors and all their photo shoots and personal changes. (Same goes for you, Donna and Kevin!)

To Lisa: You're right—there is certainly something wondrous in the floorboards here. Come visit the boat with your daughters any time.

To Alice, Steve, Casey, Lauren, Nell, Linnay, Brookie, Eliz, Shmoo, Bonnie, Justina, Amy, Shavonda, Heidi, Lizzie, Mimi and DJ: Your love means everything to me and lifts our family. Thank you forever and always.

To the Sage and Winkleman families: I still can't believe that we fit the entire crew inside this house! Thank you for your encouragement of our funny little world.

To Mom, Dad, and Jess: You showed me that people, experiences, and love are what matter in this world. I can never, ever thank you enough for that gift, which I am so lucky to be able to pass on to West. I have felt incredibly supported and heard throughout my entire life. You have given me the world by giving me your love. Thank you.

To my son, West—I love you with every cell of my body, and am in complete awe of how you've transformed our home into the happiest place I could ever imagine. You are so loved, sweet boy.

To my husband, Adam—No one else can do what you do. Thank you for your passion, your strength, and your patience. West, StanLee, Sophee, and I are the luckiest beings on Earth because of you.

And to every person who has read our family's blog, visited our Instagram, waved to us along the Venice Beach canals, or cheered in support while passing us on our cargo bike: I appreciate all of your kind words. Thank you for filling our lives with such a unique joy, and for celebrating daily with us here in our tiny home.

IMAGE CREDITS

All illustrations by Magdalena Zolnierowicz. Title lettering by Lindsay Hollinger. Storyboard illustration by Conor Buckley.

All photos courtesy of the author with exception of the following:

Yayo Ahumada for The Chalkboard: 141 Sebastian Artz: p. 10 (introduction) Lincoln Barbour: 202–204 A Beautiful Mess: 106 Justina Blakeney: 117 Kat Borchart: 001 Katie Branch: 161 Hilton Carter: 077–079 Dabito: 065 DeuceCitiesHenHouse.com: 027 Fantastic Frank Real Estate: 158 Getty Images: 130, 206 Lily Glass: 023, 046 (above; straw bags hanging on wall), 057, 095, 107, 166 (left; dog in doorway), 199 (right; wooden dollhouse) Deborah Gordon: 200 Lindsay Hollinger: 199 (above left; Whitney with baby) Ana Kamin for Apartment Therapy: 070 Lauren Logan/Paige Morse Creative: 018 Mavis the

Airstream: 171–173 Jenna Peffley (products and styled by Fragments Identity): p. 16 (Living chapter opener) Joey Puterbaugh: 054, 055, 056, 176 (top and bottom) Regan Baker Design: 080 Kayla Sampson of Dulcet Creative: 140 Sarah Sherman Samuel: 155 Christine Sandrock: 002 Christina Shirley of Stella Blue Gallery: 131–133 Shutterstock: 019, 075, 092, 118 SpechtArchitects.com: 084 Stocksy: 013, 021, 045, 069, 110, 122, 125, 127, 159, 163, 167, 177, 189, 209, 219, 226, 227 Will Strawser: 017 courtesy of Heather Tierney of The Butcher's Daughter: 086 Sara Toufali: 224 Marisa Vitale: front cover, back cover, p. 15 (top; Whitney with family) Monica Wang: 042, 152, p. 202 (Bathing chapter opener) Angie Wendricks of County Road Living: 114–116, 228–230

PUBLISHER ACKNOWLEDGMENT

Weldon Owen would like to thank Lisa Atwood, Lesley Bruynesteyn, Lisa Marietta, and Marisa Solís for their editorial expertise, and Kevin Broccoli for indexing.

weldonowen

PRESIDENT & PUBLISHER   Roger Shaw

ASSOCIATE PUBLISHER   Mariah Bear

SVP, SALES & MARKETING   Amy Kaneko

SENIOR EDITOR   Lucie Parker

ASSOCIATE EDITOR   Molly O'Neil Stewart

PROJECT MANAGER   Katherine Pearson

CREATIVE DIRECTOR   Kelly Booth

ART DIRECTOR   Lorraine Rath

DESIGNER   Jennifer Durrant

PRODUCTION DIRECTOR   Michelle Duggan

PRODUCTION MANAGER   Sam Bissell

PRODUCTION DESIGNER   Howie Severson

IMAGING MANAGER   Don Hill

Copyright © 2018 Weldon Owen International

1045 Sansome Street Suite 100

San Francisco, CA 94111

www.weldonowen.com

Printed and bound in China

ISBN: 978-1-68188-294-9

10 9 8 7 6 5 4 3 2
2018 2019 2020 2021 2022

Library of Congress Cataloging-in-Publication Data
Names: Morris, Whitney Leigh, author.
Title: Small space style : because you don't have to live large to live
    beautifully / Whitney Leigh Morris of the Tiny Canal Cottage.
Description: San Francisco, CA : Weldon Owen, 2018.
Identifiers: LCCN 2018033725 | ISBN 9781681882949 (hardback)
Subjects: LCSH: Small rooms--Decoration. | Small houses. | BISAC: HOUSE &
    HOME / Decorating. | HOUSE & HOME / Do-It-Yourself / General.
Classification: LCC NK2117.S59 M67 2018 | DDC 745.4--dc23
LC record available at https://lccn.loc.gov/2018033725